SY 0115519 9

The Richness of Art Education

KU-429-359

ST. MARY'S UNIVERSITY COLI
A COLLEGE OF THE QUEENS UNIVE

Tel. 028 902682⁴
Web site www.stmarys-
email: ¹⁴

Fine⁵

EDUCATIONAL FUTURES
RETHINKING THEORY AND PRACTICE
Volume 23

Series Editors
Michael A. Peters
University of Illinois at Urbana-Champaign, USA

Editorial Board

Michael Apple, *University of Wisconsin-Madison, USA*
Miriam David, *Institute of Education, London University, UK*
Cushla Kapitzke, *Queensland University of Technology, Australia*
Simon Marginson, *University of Melbourne, Australia*
Mark Olssen, *University of Surrey, UK*
Fazal Rizvi, *University of Illinois at Urbana-Champaign, USA*
Linda Tuahwai Smith, *University of Waikato, New Zealand*
Susan Robertson, *University of Bristol, UK*

Scope
This series maps the emergent field of educational futures. It will commission books on the futures of education in relation to the question of globalisation and knowledge economy. It seeks authors who can demonstrate their understanding of discourses of the knowledge and learning economies. It aspires to build a consistent approach to educational futures in terms of traditional methods, including scenario planning and foresight, as well as imaginative narratives, and it will examine examples of futures research in education, pedagogical experiments, new utopian thinking, and educational policy futures with a strong accent on actual policies and examples.

The Richness of Art Education

Howard Cannatella

SENSE PUBLISHERS
ROTTERDAM / TAIPEI

A C.I.P. record for this book is available from the Library of Congress.

ISBN 978-90-8790-607-8 (paperback)
ISBN 978-90-8790-608-5 (hardback)
ISBN 978-90-8790-609-2 (e-book)

Published by: Sense Publishers,
P.O. Box 21858, 3001 AW
Rotterdam, The Netherlands
http://www.sensepublishers.com

Printed on acid-free paper

All Rights Reserved © 2008 Sense Publishers

No part of this work may be reproduced, stored in a retrieval system, or transmitted in any form or by any means, electronic, mechanical, photocopying, microfilming, recording or otherwise, without written permission from the Publisher, with the exception of any material supplied specifically for the purpose of being entered and executed on a computer system, for exclusive use by the purchaser of the work.

TABLE OF CONTENTS

Preface   vii

Introduction   ix

1. MIMESIS AS KNOWLEDGE PRODUCTION   1
   Plato and Aristotle

2. ART AS EXPERIENCE   33
   John Dewey

3. ART AS THE BASIS OF EDUCATION   49
   Herbert Read

4. LANGUAGE GAMES AND RULE FOLLOWING   65
   Ludwig Wittgenstein

5. EXPERIENCE-KNOWLEDGE AND THE MORAL
   WORLD OF ART EDUCATION   87
   Louis Arnaud Reid

6. THE INDIVIDUAL VISION   99
   Maurice Merleau-Ponty

References   117

PREFACE

With the renewed interest in the importance to all our futures of creativity and innovation, there's been much public discussion in recent years about art education and its special value – education to art and education through art, to adapt Herbert Read's famous distinction. But the tone of voice in these public debates has usually been rhetorical, and the emphasis has tended to be on advocacy rather than research, assertion rather than argument, on unexamined assumptions.

The Richness of Art Education explores – with a wealth of examples from art, literature, philosophy and education – some deep perspectives on the distinctive contribution made by teachers of art: these perspectives include – in chronological order – 'mimesis' (from the ancient Greeks), 'art as experience', 'art and general education', 'art and language games', 'the moral world of art education' and 'the individual vision'. What unites them, throughout the book, is Howard Cannatella's seriousness of purpose, the clarity with which he presents each perspective, and his evident commitment to making them useful to practising teachers. The Richness of Art Education is in the end a guide to practice.

Those of us who teach in art rooms and art schools need this book. I wish it had been available when I was starting out.

PROFESSOR SIR CHRISTOPHER FRAYLING
OCTOBER 2008

INTRODUCTION

The aim of this book is to bring to life in a fresh and constructive way art education. It is a unique inquiry that examines some of the furtherance of teaching in the arts. Each chapter addresses an important issue about arts education and investigates some of the challenges of teaching that these issues raise. The theory and practice of the arts in education is covered throughout. Seminal figures have been chosen for their different understanding of arts education, whose respective thoughts have contributed something special, enduring and formidable. Their writings in general form part of the formative impulse of what is upstanding about arts education. The selected themes of the book are designed to enhance our sense of the particular and wider concerns that affect art teaching today, to offer more clarity about them and to spur further discussion. In this text, much is debated about the world of teaching in the arts, its cultural work, understanding, value, and daily faculties. With attention being paid on the one hand to primary, secondary and undergraduate teaching and on the other to policy and theory in education, the book is an attempt to reclaim and reinforce the relevance of the arts in our schools, colleges and universities.

Investigated are ideas concerning the traditional, novel, contemporary, and befitting notions of art in education. In teaching ways the book discusses: knowledge production in the arts, morality in the arts, meaning in arts, the politics of art, rules of art, the nature of art, the importance of art, the ordinariness of art, the language of art, the making of art, children's art, representation in art, expression in art, perception, cognition, imagination and the body in art, understanding in art, experience in art, the dissatisfaction of art education, student centeredness in art, the syllabus in art, the philosophy of art, the social and the other in art, aesthetic education and human becoming in art. In offering a critique of some major figures and their themes, the book demonstrates the rewards of art education in a creative, intellectual and practical fashion. These chapters represent some of the most exciting, vital, and finest work on arts education. A sense of history and a sense of the present are discussed to serve the teaching of art. The depth and variety of the topics involved suggest something of the lustre of arts education that may further suggest that the arts, as John White puts it, are one of the inexhaustible features of human well-being (White, 1995).

All of the figures chosen have conceptualised and expanded the theory of learning and teaching in the arts in ways that have applied relevance for contemporary practice in art education at all levels. A few of the names on first sight may seem an unusual inclusion but I am optimistic that by reading about them here one will feel there is justification for their insertion in this work. Not just the regular and normal, but also the perplexing, moving, distinctive, and sophisticated acts of art practice in education are debated as well. Attention is paid to the poetic, performing, and visual arts. Between the chapters there exist various overlaps, agreements, connections, and tensions as well. Yet this is a book that is not dominated by a single thesis; rather it canvasses a wide range of different perspectives that seek to wrestle with the complexity of art education from substantially different points of view. Although the list of renowned figures is short in number, I have wanted to heed the warning of Francesco Cordasco (1987, p. vii) of producing a "biographical digest without any scholarly underpinnings and without any real assistance" to the teacher.

What is good about the arts is provoked and questioned throughout the book from a variety of positions. Some of the common teaching input that is essential to the success of the arts in education is imparted. Whatever chapter one chooses to read first, each renowned thinker isolates issues poignant to the profession of art education. The book does not aim to convey a prescribed body of knowledge and skills for the teaching of art, but it does attempt to convey some of its specialised understanding, verity, and erudition. Like a journey, this volume takes us on a voyage to re-examine some of the landscape of arts education. It is a study that gives an overview of a few of the well-meaning benchmarks in arts education. What these writers bring to the table of art education cannot be dismissed lightly because each one of them has something to say of special value which challenges us. It is hoped that the reader will grasp a sense of the validating power and practicum of arts education. My thoughts on each theme, is an attempt to open up, state, and discover the industry, prudent truths and analysis that make art education such a primary subject in education generally.

The reader will discern in the book how art education is engaging, enlarging, and redefining its professional practices. This inquiry reviews in more ways than one, how art education, is an essential part of human flourishing. Each chapter is not intended to give a comprehensive account of the breadth of each figure's work but rather to act as a guide to some of their thinking which it is hoped can be used to assist teaching in art education and decide policy. As Marion Richardson (1948, p11–12) mentions in relation to her reservations about her art teacher training course: "It could not be that the mere ability to copy crabs' claws, bathroom taps, umbrellas, ivy leaves, or even the casts from the antique to which these elementary things were the prelude, constituted art" . We have all experienced a similar doubt perhaps when teaching art, and in reading this book there can be an ennobling interchange about such thoughts that represent a kind of self-respect and modesty that is a reflection of oneself as one is. When thoughts push up from below they can have a marked effect on one's teaching practice. The thinkers in this book are particularly good at capitalising on such thoughts. They are all practitioners and theorists of vision, tenacity, artistry, intellectual force, political awareness, unerring kindness, psychological acuteness, extensive teaching experience, and comprehensive knowledge.

The space of learning in art, its teaching methods and the lives of those who learn from it are further concerns of this manuscript. I trust that the words spoken here will make the reader feel that as a teacher in the arts one is not alone, that the book gives real comfort, joy, and precise challenges for teaching and that it establishes that the present history of art education is potent, creative, curious, purposeful, caring, erudite and pertinent to the world and a measure of it. In an uneasy world, this is a book that dares to think differently about art education in sensitive, penetrative, and expansive ways.

HOWARD CANNATELLA CERT ED, MA RCA, PHD

MIMESIS AS KNOWLEDGE PRODUCTION

Plato and Aristotle

"Why should man be obeyed more than any other animal? Is it because, as Plato answered Neocles, he alone of all animals can count? Or is it because he is the only animal that believes in gods? Or is it because he is the most imitative (for it is for this reason that he can learn)?" (Aristotle, 1984c, Book XXX, p. 1504).

Abstract

Ordinarily, if one is looking to find out exactly when and how art educational theory got started; if one is looking to find out what theory of art has had the biggest and longest effect on art education; if one wants to avoid the frivolous and the lightweight; if one has a yearning for depth and reliability; if one is searching for those whose thoughts on art in education have been substantial and if one feels it helps teaching to understand the subject theoretically and practically, then all these points taken together converge on Plato and Aristotle.

Introduction

This is the longest chapter in the book for the simple reason that Plato and Aristotle are two gigantic heavy weights in the field of art educational theory and practice. Their critical claims, though very different in kind, have been decisive for art education. Our investigation has three aims. Firstly, to outline a teaching perspective of mimesis with practical implications; secondly, to discuss Plato's reservations concerning mimesis in art education; and thirdly, to justify why Aristotle's approach has "elementary validity" (Gadamer, 1998, p. 97).

What specialised teaching knowledge of art does an art teacher need to have to go into a class or studio to teach children and adults? One branch of the teacher's distinctive teaching knowledge in art education that we are going to discuss is the notion of mimesis. We may have forgotten the importance of mimesis in teaching, but in this chapter we are going to resurrect this concept in order to show its specialised knowledge and significance. While we all have our preferences—abstraction, constructionism, fauvism, romanticism, surrealism, technological art, post-modernism, rock, ballet, free dancing, or jazz. I believe that there are sound educational reasons why the teaching of mimesis in art education should be a necessary feature of the syllabus of art. However much we know about different art movements, and however good we are at teaching their strengths, we cannot be teaching art properly without the inclusion of imitation in art.

Undoubtedly, imitation in art education has what some people strongly dislike about this practice: a traditional language of art. I believe we should not feel apologetic for this in the slightest because being part of a mimetic tradition gives art education a corpus like no other. We can trace this tradition back to one of its impulses in the famous Palaeolithic Lascaux Caves in France. The age of representation had begun when the artists in the Lascaux Caves and elsewhere influenced the course of history and the arena of art. The world we all live in realised long ago how it could usefully deploy artistic representations to create perspectives of different times and places. However dynamic art in the present is, we can still feel connections to past art because we can "feel the movement of life" (Gadamer, 1998, p. 116) in these works due to the doctrine of imitation as representation. The narrative of life constantly changes, but the realistic brilliance of imitation as representation has sought to move with it. Being part of a tradition of great achievement in art education with the irreplaceable Lascaux Caves to refer to, for example, does not necessarily mean that imitation in art has been unadventurous. Those who have taken this stand have not understood the compulsiveness, *raison d'être,* and life-serving significance of this tradition. We can also easily avoid the charge that mimesis is conservative thinking and any argument with it, when we can show how and why mimesis is coextensive with its past but is still in diverse ways constantly facing the present and the future (Gadamer, 1998, p. 9). Few teachers would question this given the history of art teaching and the manner in which mimesis has developed. A random snapshot image of the present from different regions of the world might suggest that artists such as Paula Rego, R.B Kitaj, Cindy Sherman, Alan Feltus, Andrea Martinelli, Ron Mueck, Philip Pearlstein, William Beckman, Jean-Luc Blanc, Liu Maoshan, Cheng Shifa, Xu Lele, Bao Chenchu, Alan Bennett, Czeslaw Milosz, Katerina Anghelaki-Rooke, and Seamus Heaney are all sharing, to various degrees, the art tradition of mimesis.

With the idea that mimesis involves a tradition in art we are indicating a way of how we can use it to our advantage in teaching. Having an illustrious tradition of imitation in art means we can enter the past, as in the case of the Lascaux Caves, but carry this past forward with the sensibilities of the present. The tradition is therefore kept alive albeit in a fashion that designates our own world in it today. This tradition involves in art education mimetically, four vital forces which we see present in the Lascaux Caves. The first is that we are nothing without a "memory and recollective appropriation" (Gadamer, 1998, p. 10). The second is the power of art to penetrate deeply into life to produce refined images of it. Third, we find the child's "spirit lies in the ability to move within the horizon of an open future and an unrepeatable past" (Gadamer, 1998, p. 10). Fourth, the "nerve to get close enough for a collaboration to start" (Berger, 2002, p. 16).

Alden Nowlan's poem, below, invites the kind of representation that Aristotle refers to in his *Poetics*, disclosing the human scale of life which elevates art education.

"She hugs me now, this retarded woman, and I hug her.
We are brother and sister, father and daughter,
mother and son, husband and wife.
We are lovers. We are two human beings
Huddled together for a little while by the fire
In the Ice Age, two hundred thousand years ago" (Nowlan, 2004, p. 138–9).

The figurative, in a form that tells stories concerning people, their lives and their worlds, is an ancient one. In a letter that Joanne Gonzalez sent to the editor Neil Ashley about the poetry book *Staying Alive,* Joanne writes of her mother: "She is 90, and blind. I had just bought *Staying Alive* and began reading it to her. I do not exaggerate to say she was transformed. She asked to hold the book, and pressed it against her forehead. She chose life today because of your book" (Gonzalez, 2004, p. 20). Perhaps this is all the proof we need as teachers for the relevance of mimetic art and anyone who thinks this is not enough is missing something precious about humanity itself. Of course one might reply that a ninety-year-old woman is a very different person to a nine-year-old child, but any child can be rejuvenated by a story, poem, song, dance, or painting in exactly this way.

Being part of a historical tradition also means we can choose contemporary artists for teaching examples. The teacher does not need to go far to find revealing material of this sort for there are hundreds of short stories to be found in most school libraries with such Compulsive titles as: "The Rascally Cake," "The Day I Swapped My Dad For Two Goldfish," "Scritch Scratch," "The Wheels On the Bus," "Bat Loves the Night," "Captain Underpants," "Dancing Dreams," "The Killer Cat," "Thomas Knew There Were Pirates Living in the Bathroom," and "George's Marvellous Medicine" which speak to us in mimetic ways of the drama of life. Whether it is Shakespeare's *Tempest,* Francis Hodgson Burnett's *The Secret Garden,* L. M. Montgomery's *Anne of Green Gables,* Helen Keller's *The Story of My Life* or more recently Alan Bennett's *The History Boys,* the issue of teaching imitation in art is also part of a culture that is changing. What can be learnt from Shakespeare and from more recent works like Anthony Horowitz's *Stormbreaker,* Jacqueline Wilson's *Love Lessons,* Louis Sachar's *Holes* and Ted Hughes' *Iron Man* can contribute to the mix of mimesis to make the culture of one's own youth less of an issue for students. When ten-year-olds are learning in their school orchestra to play the theme tunes for Star Wars, James Bond, Harry Potter, the Pink Panther and the Simpsons, then the children can be inspired beyond their years. The playwright Alan Bennett in his diary for the film production of *The History Boys* writes: "The best moments in reading are when you come across something— a thought, a feeling, a way of looking at things—which you had thought special and particular to you" (Bennett, 2006, p. xxi).

Teaching mimetically in art connects to the expressed manner representation and enactment portrays life. It can teach the student to become attuned with a past and a present: (1) "Without this historical sensibility we would probably be unable to perceive the precise compositional mastery displayed by earlier art" (Gadamer, 1998, p. 11). (2) Mimetic practice aims to help the student achieve representations and enactments that are superior in perception. (3) To construct art so that it displays understanding and meaning in recognisable and universal ways (an Aristotelian point we will come back to discuss). (4) Mimesis unfolds naturally from the child and is important for their well-being and learning, as Aristotle compellingly writes in Book Four of his *Poetics*. (5) Because it is part of a tradition that has been enormously creative over the centuries, there is a substantial body of practice with plenty of material to draw from for the teacher, such as the unmistakable imagery of Botticelli, Rembrandt, Piero della Francesa, Picasso, or Francis Bacon.

Now, Plato was aware that mimesis as a theory was in the making at the time he wrote the *Republic* (approximately 360.BC). He contributed enormously to the debate and is singled out as the "first Greek thinker to explore the idea of mimetic art in a theoretically extensive and probing manner" (Halliwell, 2002, p. 37). Plato's arguments against imitation in art remain as salient as ever. While there is more than meets the eye with Plato, no one has mounted a serious criticism against art education as severe as Plato's theory and it would surely be a sign of neglect, if not stupidity, if art education ignored it. We have to grasp something of how correctly, and incorrectly, Plato perceives art in education mimetically because if we do not we are always open to his challenge that there is an inherent feebleness about art education.

Why do we still value mimesis in art education? This may also be due to the fact that its productive knowledge has shown itself to be versatile and incorrigible for the world. In the hands of the common and the most talented alike it has touched people's lives deeply through the centuries and continues to do so. It was not just the rich, famous, or intellectual elite that came to see the plays of Sophocles or Shakespeare. It is natural, as Elaine Scarry mentions, to want to replicate and reproduce what the eyes see as beautiful (Scarry, 2000). In alphabetical order only and to various degrees acting, architecture, crafts, dance, drama, fashion, film, graphic design, literature, music, photography, poetry, product design, and sculpture have all advanced artistically because of different conceptions of mimetic art thinking and teaching. "Mimesis, in all its variations, has quite simply proved to be the most long-lasting, widely held and intellectually accommodating of all theories of art in the West" (Halliwell, 2002, p. 5–6). Yet, let us not think that the power of mimesis rests on its flexibility and versatility alone, neither of which is worth very much if we cannot feel the mettle of its seduction influencing the fabric of our human becoming.

I

To get us feeling *au fait* with the concept of mimesis in art education we will start with a sketch of the factors that affect the pedagogy of it. Some of these points will be expanded later in the chapter. With this background knowledge up front, I feel we will be in a better position to then take account of Plato and Aristotle in our final sections.

Depending on the type of media involved, the teaching of mimesis is guided by enactment or representational traits. In the case of drama, enactment is requisite, and in painting, representation is required. Certainly, a gamut of differences can exist between drama, painting, poetry, music, and sculpture but Aristotle in his *Poetics* shows how enactment and representation can intertwine. Enactment involves student performances in drama, dance or music. Mimetic performances are enactments with the relevant resemblance and drama of life. We can see drama in dance as we can see drama in a play. Reading poetry in a class will sometimes require a performance that is spoken with a rhythm and an inflexion akin to the style and meaning of the poem. Traditionally, painting and sculpture are not thought of as performances *per se*. In fine art practice images appear frozen in gestural and inspired representative ways. This might be a Christmas scene, a game of rugby, or two lovers kissing, a horse, an apple, or building sand castles on the beach. Recently, sculptural installations and video art recordings have begun using performances as a way to extend further the vernacular of art. These points aside, enactment may be depicting and representing events just as much as a poem, painting, or sculpture can.

Whatever is going to be an imitative project for students to tackle in an art class or studio, we can be certain that it must exhibit a "reference to or substitute for the real existence of something" (Gadamer, 1998, p. 35) in a picture, image, or as a performance. Imitation expresses realism as art and not realism, as Cora Diamond (1996, p. 40) explicates, simply by deduction, by statistics or by meta-analysis. We recognise mimesis in art in perceptual ways. Mimesis in art education exploits the expressible in enactment and representation (Gadamer, 1998, p. 96) by drawing from the student's contact and the life they lead. In one sense nothing has changed. Art education is still concerned with events in the world as it was in the past, and as Plato and Aristotle surmised in earlier times, mimesis then and now follows a tradition of imitating life. This means that mimetic representations-enactments in art education re-create imaginatively true-to-life experiences, events, sounds, and images. From Plato, I take it that a mimetic representation-enactment is modelled on the incident it is made to look like, and from Aristotle I take it also that a mimetic representation-enactment relates further to "this person being so-and-so' (Aristotle, 1984b, Book 4, p. 2318). The imitative process of art education that Gadamer detects in relation to Heidegger's *The Origin of the Work of Art,* can provoke the revealing, unconcealing, and manifesting compulsion of existence, as well as the concealing and sheltering aspects of life (Gadamer, 1998, p. 34). Homer's *Iliad* is one example of this art and the seventeenth-century painting by Velázquez's *Las Meninas* may be another.

Mimetic practice in art education "should not violate the laws of probability" (Gadamer, 1998, p. 94), and, as Gadamer exegetically explains, representation traditionally had the belief in the idealising capacity of the 'imitation of nature'. The Greek sculptor Polykleitos idealised his figures but would we say the same for Sophocles' *Antigone*? Idealising or not, art education mimetically demands "legibility" (Gadamer, 1998, p. 96), so that the student's artwork becomes 'readable'. We can say that our student produced different mimetic representations-enactments of their cat and did so through a range of songs, paintings, poems, sculptures, acting, dance movements, and stories. Imitation of nature, imitative realism, cultural realism, modernist realism, native realism, post-modern realism and historical styles of representation and enactment, for example, may serve to suggest all kinds of comparable notions of mimetic creativity in art education.

Playing, reading, having conversations and dialogue, forming friendships, completing assignments, helping others, and going on visits, adventures and journeys are the kinds of experiences that extend how children encounter themselves and the world. We encounter ourselves when "the world is what we see" (Merleau-Ponty, 2000, p. 3). These commonplace encounters, however variegated they may be, reverberate with the reveries of childhood (Bachelard, 1971). The construction process of art in education begins from this world and the characters, incidents and journeys that provoke such abundant pictures full of life, relate in part from "the joy of recognition" (Bachelard, 1971, p. 99) which comes from understanding the recognition (Aristotle, 1984b, Book 4). A misrepresentation would be a performance or product that we could not recognise relevantly 'as' something; the "knowledge that it implies" (Gadamer, 1998, p. 99). Mimetic construction is the result of the child's work and is not something that exists in the world before the child creates it in representative ways (Nehamas, 1982, p. 62). Mimesis in art education is synonymous with recognition but these recognitions, as Aristotle enumerated in his *Poetics* are produced by a poetic culture.

Our teacher asks: 'Who can recognise what this story is about?' 'Can you recognise in the picture the big bad wolf?' Our teacher says: 'children, let us see if we can dance with the movement of a tree in mind'. 'When we recognise that this is a story about rabbits can we also recognise how it is being delicately portrayed?' 'It is difficult to see what you are depicting here, Ian, and this makes it difficult for me to recognise what it is'. Our student might say: 'I recognise where I have gone wrong', 'I recognise that I need to improve my dancing technique', 'I recognise that the resemblance is not very good here', 'I recognise that if I mix blue and yellow, I will make green' and 'I recognise what this is about, miss'. Recognition, Aristotle proposes, leads to understanding and "we delight to view the most realistic representations of them in art" (Aristotle, 1984, book 4, p. 2318). When children dress up and disguise themselves (Gadamer, 1998, p. 98) we are not supposed to see the child but what the child represents in the disguise "recognition confirms and bears witness to the fact that mimetic behaviour makes something present" (Gadamer, 1998, p. 99). Another reason for "the delight in seeing the picture is that one is at the same time learning—gathering the meaning of the things" (Aristotle, 1984b, Book 4, p. 2318). Children contrive what so-and-so is by noting what is real about so-and-so, even when it is a pantomime performance of *Jack and the Bean Stalk*. The knowledge production that goes into making what so-and-so is becomes a factor in the child's learning process since it determines, as Aristotle declares (Aristotle, 1984b, Book 2), the realism to represent people, for example, as either better or worse. Therefore, one of the mimetic teaching issues in art education "consists precisely in the recognition of the represented in the representation" (Gadamer, 1998, p. 99).

How do children learn to recognise and understand by imitating? By the time they come to school, children already have an informed understanding of representation and enactment. In make-believe activities they will substitute a stick for a horse, a cardboard box for a rocket, they can produce a painting of their rabbit at home and can possibly imitate the voice of Harry Potter. When the child substitutes a stick for a horse, how is the visual resemblance operating? Alan Goldman (2003, p. 198) remarks that visual resemblance can operate in all sorts of ways. How does a stick resemble a horse? It is in the social acting and playing that a stick can be used to express a horse with a rider on top. The relevant resemblance, as Goldman contends, cannot be a stick corresponding to a horse, as a stick and a horse have very little resemblance in common. What convinces the teacher of a relevant resemblance here is how the stick is used in a performance to present a horse with a rider on top. We see the stick as a horse with a rider on top because the child's acting mimics imaginatively some of the actions and features that are fictionally real enough to be perceived as a horse with a rider on top.

Mimetic practice is constrained by recognition, resemblance, and familiarity. This involves having a realistic attitude about the knowledge production of art and its effect. Rather like Aristotle, Diamond insists that a story is "unrealistic if the plot proceeds by a series of improbable events" (Diamond, 1996, p. 41). The mimetic construction focuses on what Aristotle thought as the probable inclination of what something should look like or be performed 'as'. We judge what something should look like or be performed as in art education, when the child's "product has a special nature of its own" (Gadamer, 1998, p. 125). As previously stated, it is not just the 'knowledge that it implies' but whether mimetically it has a 'special nature of its own'. It must have its own style and vision, its own way of playing. A child's or adult's mimetic realisation that so-and-so is a horse would have to have a significance beyond simply recognising that it had four legs, a head and a tail. Franz Marc's *Red Horses* (1911) and *Blue Horse* (1911) are examples of the elevation that Aristotle speaks of in his *Poetics* where recognition is being transformed into something which has a defined and superior poetic sense to it. Marc's horses express a different kind of lushness, coolness, and relaxed stance which explicate a primitive and rhythmic representing image of them.

Teaching imitation in art aims to reveal "precisely the real essence of things" (Gadamer, 1998, p. 99). Here are some examples of how this might be produced: (1) "Sheep have an entirely different feeling from, say, horses, or cats or dogs" (Moore and Hedgecoe, 1986, p. 282). (2) "We pass trees hundreds of times, but ask someone to draw a tree—how much have they seen" (Moore and Hedgecoe, 1986, p. 158). (3) "One might ask why in this drawing does he make that black behind the shoulder; the reason is that it forces the shoulder out from the background" (Caro, 2006, p. 116). (4): "As is common in Moore's life drawings, here a low viewpoint gives greater weight to the legs and lower torso, and much less to the girlish head" (Stallabrass, 2006, p. 104). A fifth example, is how mimetically to support in teaching the fact that a child can look at a robot carpet cleaner and think that it has a hidden death ray in it. Something tells me the child is right and that this too may be part of the essence of the robot's magical power when an object haunts the child in fantastical self-imposed ways.

"Recognition, as understood by Aristotle, presupposes the continuing existence of a binding tradition that is intelligible to all and in which we can encounter ourselves" (Gadamer, 1998, p. 100). This 'binding tradition' that Gadamer is speaking of here simply means the tradition of producing meaningful recognitions. The second part of this quote suggests that the teacher should explore with the students how they want to reveal their world so that their imitations are recognisable images of the world but are more than trivial enactments and representations of it.

Our culture introduces us to legends, fantasies, fairy tales, underworlds, quests, larger- than-life characters, terrible things, heroic deeds, ritual, magic, witches, pirates, dragons, and unicorns. *The Arabian Nights, Beowulf, Robin Hood, King Arthur and the Knights of the Round Table, Doctor Who, The Odyssey* by Homer and various works in Hans Christian Andersen, Roald Dahl, J.K. Rowling, Jill Murphy, William Blake, Brueghel the Elder, J.R. Tolkien, Dean Swift, Zbigniew Herbert, Miguel de Cervantes, Egyptian, Mayan and African art offer dreaming perspectives which seem to confirm why Aristotle thought, namely that art is more elevated truth than history is.

The critical powers of art admonishing the tragic existence of life as we encounter it can promote well-being, as Nietzsche argued in the *Birth of Tragedy*. Aristotle in his *Poetics* explains at some length why tragedy is no ordinary pleasure because it hinges on a spectacle which transmits an immutable understanding of the world. Full of passion, sentiment, experience, horror, struggle and healing, tragedy in art education invites us to consider how destructive, unreal, painful, and devious we all are. Theatre as staged drama "may be painful to see" (Aristotle, 1984, Book 4, p. 2318) due to the devastation the play portrays. The representation of which can still be enjoyable because of its insight into events and views that connect to the action of the persons concerned. We can become animated by the play's realistic presentation when it is never mean or debased.

Most representation in Classic Greek sculpture is an attempt to idealise the human body. For the sculptor, grasping the ideal through the senses in figurative ways in order to convey what was then thought of as an ultimate conception of being in the world, meant exploring representational images of self-control, serenity, harmony, 'perfection', and the human form as a thing of beauty. The ideal form is triumphantly schematised into an ethical ideal of heroic bodies, symbolising self-determination, worldliness, physical union, spirit, and freedom. These traits we see exhibited further in the work of Dürer, Michelangelo, Raphael, Poussin, Delacroix, Ingres, Matisse, and Cézanne. In other ways, too, we are touched by how Henry Moore idealises mother and child images in his sculptures to such an extent that we are humbled by them. Hegel remarks that one of the issues of art as idealisation is to convert the "visible surface into an eye, which is the seat of the soul and brings the spirit into appearance" (Hegel, 1988, Vol. 1, p. 153). It is a common feature of all the arts to idealise and children are particularly good at representing larger-than-life images.

We encounter ourselves sometimes behaving romantically, which we often view as idealised love. When children paint a flower or a bird, when they dance to a song or when they write about their sister or brother, mother or father, their dog or a friend, what passes in such representations may be exactly this kind of idealised love. A world of feeling and inner life, as Hegel put it in his *Lectures on Fine Art*. The Romantic Movement is often credited with championing a world of spontaneity, liberty, passion, delight, affection, imagination, emotion, sensuality, and personal conviction. Some noted examples in less than puritanical ways are in the world of literature, Wordsworth, Coleridge, Charlotte, Anne and Emily Brontë, Byron, Mary Shelly, Keats; and among the painters Turner, Géricault, Goya, and Casper David Friedrich. Romanticism continues to influence countless poets, prose writers, painters, and dancers today.

Humour is important to children's intellectual and moral well being. It comforts them and can arouse an exalting and enlightening self. We know that the funniest stories are sometimes the best stories to discuss with children. A funny story may be poignant and absurd at the same time. The generous, vigorous, peculiar, bizarre, strange, silly, courageous, kind, challenging, intelligent, and fantastical nature of these stories represents the splendid spirit of children. A cheerful confidence can come from reading stories that reflect the vexations and imaginations of childhood. Neil Gaiman and Dave McKean's book *The Day I Swapped my Dad for Two Goldfish* is an example of children's imagination and behaviour that has other children laughing in socially important ways. Roald Dahl stories are deliberately modest in style: plain and domestic. What is true of his stories is that they are full of astonishing, grotesque, small and gigantic figures. Tongue-in-cheek remarks, idyllic and absurd incidents, chicanery, innocence, fallibility, and comical characterisations are incisive features of his work.

We further encounter ourselves in art education through the production of 'realist' work. This idea concerns how life appears in the world to be as it is observed. John Dewey's *Art as Experience* emphasises some of these qualities. The work of Aleksandr Solzhenitsyn, Émile Zola, Mark Twain, George Orwell, Anne Frank and many of the writers already mentioned in this chapter manifest this quality. Realism refers sometimes to the surface appearance of things, the perception of things and the event or actual incidents that happen in everyday existence. To recognise what it is a picture of, argues, Crispin Sartwell (1992, p. 354), is to note the realism in it.

Our modern urban culture with its consumerist lifestyles, politics, and the entertainment world can become the inspiration for a teenager's poem, dance, craft, product design or sculpture piece. In some ways, pop art is what most children are familiar with when, for example, they exchange the latest fantasy graphic game cards in the playground, the computer games they play, the text messages they send, their dress sense, the food they eat, the TV and films they watch, the posters they have on their bedroom walls and the books they read. Pop art is youth culture: colourful, fashion conscious, loud and well adapted to the pleasures of life. Vibrant and trendsetting pop art can command a strong sensory vividness to reflect back on the social strata and politics in contemporary society.

In all of the categories above, children portray themselves in art education as the subjects they are. It is not uncommon in art education to combine realism with fantasy, or idealism with realism, or further still, romanticism, idealism, realism, tragedy and science fiction into a single story. How would we classify Otto Dix: as simply a realist painter? How would we classify Ted Hughes's book *Iron Man*: as science fiction or realist work? Would we describe Shakespeare as a romantic, satirist, realist, idealist, tragedian, or fantasist? His *Tempest* shows signs of all these qualities. Likewise, the Swedish painter Carl Larsson painted events that appear realistic, symbolic, romantic, idealised, and with figures sometimes in mythological costumes. He would deliberately add a cat, flowers, a teapot, colours, and lighting as he saw fit to do so. Larsson's style of painting extenuated or softened the naturalistic appearances in his artwork's romantic, simple and domesticated narrative scenes. His paintings tell stories and they are dramatic, arranged, and culturally conditioned.

What we can learn from a Chinese, abstract, or decorative painting style can have an important affect on the knowledge production of mimetic construction in art education. The tradition of mimesis in art education demands creativity and from the Lascaux Caves onwards, representation and enactment continues to be receptive to multidimensional influences. Life's realities are constantly being tested, rejected, reinterpreted and developed. Mimetically, different styles in realism, romanticism, idealism, tragedy, and humour which were originally only found in a single culture are now spread widely across many cultures. The very synergy of which has helped to infuse more inter-cultural exchanges that have assisted the cross-pollinating of art forms to further open up new energetic critiques in which to express everyday events, freedoms, experiences, and meanings. However we hit upon ideas for new mimetic production in art, we may still be ready to absorb into the artwork some historical and universal claims but now in terms of a contemporary spirit that can speak in many different self-accounting ways. The world is more open to ideas, dynamic movement, imagination, and experiences than ever before.

Some might take the view that in art education "the more closely the appearance of the picture surface approaches the appearance of what it depicts" (Budd, 1996, p. 45) in the world, the more closely this fictive depiction in the picture will relate to our actual perceptions and experiences of it. The picture is supposedly analogous to what it depicts. This process can claim to mirror the real fictively. Mirroring the real fictively in this manner is not altogether appropriate for art education. A depiction like this, as Budd states, is aiming for a presentation that is a "duplicate of the model" (Nehamas, 1982, p. 62). It would be impossible to accept mere duplication as original, and just as hard to accept it as elevated representation. Students' perceptions are being tightly controlled and governed in duplication exercises. The real as fictive representation is subject to technical expertise rather than aesthetic and imaginative expertise. In this process we are asked to put aside any social, ethical, political, poetic, and emotional reactions. Nothing new or unexpected can happen. What is recuperated in the making of this duplication is the supposed surface characterisation of an object. Artistic expression relating to the reality of its time, its epoch's perceived problems and self-orientation issues, are disconnected. It is not clear to me how we can successfully teach representation in this manner when what stands in the way is human life, culture, and society. Hegel considers this kind of imitation in art as "deceptive": "the pursuit of imitation is on the same lines as the feat of the man who has taught himself to throw lentils through a small aperture without missing" (Hegel, 1975, p. 59–60).

However, it would be foolish to dismiss out of hand what is being suggested by mirroring the real fictively, because in teaching and learning these kinds of depictions do have a place. Exercises with the real as fictive in mind can be particularly helpful for students to learn, without which they will have problems knowing the physiognomic mode of understanding which can 'realistically' portray a person, place, or animal. A student has to bear in mind the types of standardised external recognitions a teacher might ask them to consider. For example, in which direction is the light coming from, whether or not this is a three-quarter view we are looking at, what colours one sees, is there foreshortening to consider in the angle and position one is painting the model from, what is in the background and in the foreground, the spatial extension of depth in the representation, tonal techniques and the more general need for the student to be aware of their immediate contact with the external world when presenting a pictorial view of the world.

The real-as-fictive representation becomes a useful exercise to articulate and construct so long as we are aware that they are personal 'sensory visions' that over-whelmingly have been exploited through the centuries by artists for other purposes. This process has value when it becomes a means to an end and there are thousands of artists using it in just this way: Jenny Saville's Rosetta 2 (2005-6), Alexis Rockman's *The Farm* (2000), and Dino Vallis' *Between Earth and Heaven* (1999). In Chinese, Indian, or African art, past and present, there are clear cultural differences in the methods which engage common artistic problems. If we take Otto Dix as a further example, we might conclude that he also mirrors the real fictively, only he does not do so in the way Budd describes it. Thus the method that Budd has outlined shows just one way we can mirror the real fictively. The mirroring of the real fictively in art education can be achieved in all kinds of ways and as we have already suggested, the student's artwork must have a 'special nature of its own', correlative with their perceptual world. We must be clear on this point, that however a figure is represented or enacted as the actually concrete realism of 'there is', the inner impulse of creation in art decides the question of the work's bewitching effects.

To teach art with only a 'duplicate of a model' in mind would be to inhibit what the child can depict. A 'duplicate of a model' contains none of the elixir of art education that we first saw being developed in the Lascaux Caves that syntactically stresses a vision of life socially engaged. While this 'duplicate of a model' may be very skilful in one sense, the operational style it promotes may cease to have meaning for the child "for it is also part of the process that we recognise ourselves as well, and all our experience of the world are ultimately ways in which we develop familiarity with the world" (Gadamer, 1998, p. 100). We will have difficulty recognising ourselves and generating any love for the world if everything we do in art education punishes or trivialises the child's vision of the world.

At primary school, the child's simple pleasures, tenderness, and affections will often lead them to create mimetically a resistance to a rigid duplicate schematisation of a model. A life of human emotion, feeling, and emancipation is more important to them. The painter and musician Paul Klee used mimetic representation in some of his artwork but his mimetic representations have painterly intelligence to them. When Klee paints a picture of the Moon or a coffee pot, he does not create a duplicate model of these objects but rather reveals something of the demeanour of these objects that reanimates our enjoyment, making us see them in a new or forgotten way. William Wordsworth suggested that the duty of poetry was "to treat of things not as they *are*, but as they *appear*; not as they exist in themselves, but as they seem to exist to the *senses* and to the *passions*" (Wordsworth, 1907, p. 944). For Wordsworth, the child who is interested in poetry must proceed from their own experiences and exultations of delight that advances the character of their living being, the inclusion of which poetry draws upon as its basic life. A child's painting of the Moon is not the beautiful Moon, but a marvellous painting of the Moon by the child. Mimetic representations in art education depend upon the child seeing for themselves the potential in things as their intimacy, enhanced human consciousness and dwelling (Bachelard, 1994).

There are a number of ways mimetic representation can be taught. We can teach it by examples ('follow me as I do this', or 'show me you can do this') or by a display of physical work in the classroom or studio. Children also learn through demonstrations, discussions, reading, performance, and slide or film shows; by following what their peers are doing, by sharing their work and thoughts with others, and by being a role model; the child learns to reconstruct and re-enact the world; assignments where "'all arts are like mirrors,' according to Alain, 'in which Man learns and recognises something of himself of which he was unaware'" (Comte-Sponville, 2005, p. 100). "What would Mozart have been without Haydn? Schubert without Beethoven? All of them without Bach?" (Comte-Sponville, 2005, p. 103) What did Manet learn from Velázquez or Monet from Manet or Francis Bacon from Velázquez? What did Seamus Heaney learn from T.S. Eliot and what did our eleven-year-old student learn from a sixteen-year-old student playing *Macbeth*?

Some of the first painting lessons that children may tackle will produce images of 'my holiday', 'my hand', 'my new dress', 'I can stand on my head', 'I have a loose tooth', "my birthday party', 'mother and father', 'we are playing in the playground', 'I caught a fish', 'playing football', 'leaves', 'castle', 'cow', 'my friend', 'trees", 'our house', 'me riding a bicycle', 'me drinking lemonade', 'zoo' and 'my bedroom with me in the bed'. They may write a story about some of these things and act out being a lion, a tree, a key, a monster, a pirate, eating a meal, or being a friend. During music and dance lessons they may learn to dance spontaneously to the rhythm of the music, to the sound of drums, thunder, water, wind, footsteps, a creaking door, and a ticking clock.

We can separate mimetic practice from other art forms when "we imagine a painting that can be understood independently of its representational status, then we imagine an abstract painting" (Scruton, 1982, p. 210). To think that it is possible to understand "Rembrandt's *Nightwatch*, for example, while being indifferent to or ignorant of its representational status is absurd" (Scruton, 1982, p. 210). For the music student who is learning to play the recorder, the teacher will say, 'play it like this', which implies a certain copying or reproduction but "musical imitation is evocative rather than exact; it conveys the idea of the thing" (Scruton, 1982, p. 211–212). Indeed, it is not copying but recognising. Our student has to demonstrate by showing and "showing points away from itself" (Gadamer, 1998, p. 128). In performance, musical imitation also requires precision. It is common to say to a student, 'express these notes like this' in order to show how the "music attracts us by a beauty intrinsic to its form" (Davies, 2005, p. 502), and the form, its figuration, is what the student learns. The student learns to react to the actions, executions, and suggestions of the teacher in closely connected ways. When music and drama are working together in songs, operas, plays, dances, and film scripts we might see representation and expression of different kinds overlapping. Equally, there is "[t]he imitation of sound by an auditory design—whether the dropping of the guillotine is imitated by pizzicato strings, as in Berlioz's Fantastic Symphony, or by an actual guillotine specifically called for in the score" (Beardsley, 1981, p. 322).

We teach mimetic representation because it takes account of the human space and the world around us. We use it to entice, bond, inspire, and find out what resonates with our students. The child's own reality and that of others expressed mimetically through art education is not just a stepping stone to other forms of artwork; it should invite creatively the provocation for further development of this art form since it can reflect, as Aristotle saw, a more philosophical basis than history (Aristotle, 1984b, Book 9, p. 2323); the flesh of existence.

The student-poet depicts a hotel in Paris but the student-actor does not depict a tragedy because their role is to enact it. The student-playwright describes a scene and the student-actor acts it out, but the student-musician does not paint Beethoven's Fifth Symphony, they learn to play it. James played Hamlet in the school play but James does not resemble Hamlet, he represents him. His acting, however, does remind the teacher that there is a striking resemblance about how he plays Hamlet and another student she remembers. Children in an art lesson are painting from a still life and have been asked to look at the dynamics of this still life set up, its abstract forms, space, tones colours, patterns, planes, rhythms, and negative shapes, for example. They are asked to use what they see to create an understanding of the still life in a representative idealised or dreaming way perhaps. Many of Matisse's interior paintings of rooms have a decorative flatness, an idiomatic colour scheme and the breakup of planes and patterns in order to make his interiors vibrate with life. Matisse uses representational devices inventively as a means to enhance the picture space and to draw our attention to the room's intimate psychological character. A sense of place and personality dictates the earnest way he uses representational qualities liberally.

If the imitative production process is to succeed in art education, as Aristotle conceives, it would have to make plain to the senses the essential attributes of the 'object' being produced-performed and the way it is revealing this in order to show "What it is and that it is" (Aristotle, 1984, Book 6, p. 1619). The child's painting is a representation and one we recognise as depicting a fox. The image the child has created draws our attention to the way they have shown the fox as being alert. In another instance they may draw an outline or a silhouette of the fox. Another child in the same class, colours in their fox painting by using mixed media materials like tissue paper, ink, water colour, and an atomizer. They may show the fox as a friend, a mother, a hunter, a wild animal, or as an inquisitive being. They may use tin cans or wire mesh to create a three-dimensional image of a fox asleep. Here the child elicits "the image from things and imaginatively project the image into things in one and the same process" (Gadamer, 1998, p. 17). The child's artwork "makes public something other than itself; it manifests something other; it is an allegory" (Heidegger, 2000, p. 145), a symbol of its own pulsation.

The poet Zbigniew Herbert in his visit to the Lascaux caves writes:
"One of the most beautiful animal portraits in history is called the 'Chinese Horse'. The name does not signify its race; it is a homage to the perfection of the drawing of the Lascaux master. A soft black contour, at once distinct and vanishing, both contains and shapes the body's mass. A short mane, like that of a circus horse, impetuous, with thundering hooves. Ochre does not fill the body; the belly and legs are white. I realised that all descriptions, all inventories are useless in the presence of this masterpiece, which displays such a blinding, obvious unity. Only poetry and fairy-tales possess the power of instant creation. One should say, 'Once upon a time, there was a beautiful horse from Lascaux'" (Herbert, 1985, p. 9–10).

II

"Let's also tell poetry that there is an ancient quarrel between it and
philosophy" (Plato, 1997b. Book 10, p. 1211).

Face-to-face and in no particular order of importance what follows in notation form is a summary of Plato's and Aristotle's thinking relating to the teaching of mimesis in art education. What is indicated in this summary is some of the dissimilarity between Plato's and Aristotle's understanding of the pedagogy of art education and the status of mimesis. Suffice to say that, although there is some agreement between these two philosophers, Aristotle's *Poetics* can be interpreted as a virtual rebuke of much of what Plato thought mimetically of art education. Plato sees the value of imitation to be of minimum worth but Aristotle sees the value of imitation to be potentially of maximum worth. From this summary we will explore further a number of these issues.

Plato

- Plato argues that the child must be trained to appreciate music, poetry and painting. The child learns "the love of order and beauty that has been moderated by education in music and poetry" (Plato, 1997b, Book 3, p. 1040). Education ought to "end in the love of the fine and the beautiful" (Plato, 1997b, Book 3, p. 1040). Education must be completed by art, argues Plato.
- Students should learn to imitate people who are virtuous "courageous, self-controlled and pious" (Plato, 1997b, Book 3, p. 1033).
- Art education aims at only an "imitation of appearance" (Plato, 1997b, Book 10, p. 1202).
- Art is concerned with likeness (Plato, 1997b, Book 6, p. 1130–31).
- An imitator in art produces likenesses which, Plato claims, are thrice removed from the truth (Plato, 1997b, Book 10, p. 1202).
- Art education involves only image making and that "is why it can produce everything" (Plato, 1997b, Book 3, p. 1202).
- Art education encourages and excels in the excitable, insubstantial and "many multicoloured imitations" (Plato, 1997b, Book 10, p. 1209).
- Plato believes that the mimetic artist is capable of deceiving "decent people" through their works of art (Plato, 1997b, Book 10, p. 1210). An imitator of art cannot know the "good or bad quality of anything" (Plato, 1997b, Book 10, p. 1206).
- Image making gratifies "the irrational part" of life (Plato, 1997b, Book 10, p. 1210).
- Plato questions whether the artist image-making mimetic skills can never be construed as being among the best things we can do in life (Plato, 1997b, Book 10, p. 1203).
- He asserts that imitation in art education reproduces what comes easiest. Appearances can be "easily produced without knowledge of the truth" (Plato, 1997b, Book 10, p. 1203).
- Innovation in art education should be frowned upon (Plato, 1997b, Book 4, p. 1056).
- Art education should be forbidden from imitating mad, dangerous or bad people (Plato, 1997b, Book 3, p. 1033).
- Plato wants to see a pure and plain style of mimetic art learning and teaching (Plato, 1997b, Book 3, p. 1034–35).
- Plato thinks that knowing (Plato, 1997b, Book 10, p. 1204) can never be achieved in art education because art education is a process of imitation. Art education is "inferior in respect to truth" (Plato, 1997b, Book 10, p. 1209). It has "no graphs of the truth," (Plato, 1997b, Book 10, p. 1205) only images of the truth. A student learns "only images and not things that are" (Plato, 1997b, Book 10, p. 1203).
- Plato is worried that if a student imitates word-for-word a narrative, for example, they may equate education with only memorisation.

- "What does painting do in each case? Does it imitate that which is as it is, or does it imitate that which appears as it appears? Is it an imitation of appearance or of truth? (Plato, 1997b, Book 10, p. 1202)"
- In the final analysis, the value of art education, for Plato, is not whether the student sings or dances beautifully but whether what is sung or danced is morally good for us (Plato, 1997, p. 1345–6).

Aristotle

- Instinctively children "delight in works of imitation" (Aristotle, 1984b, Book 4, p. 2318).
- Mimesis is a common characteristic in how we learn, and the stage for Aristotle could be a moral force.
- The formative elements of mimesis are: plot, character, diction, action, depiction, rhythm, melody, gesture, expression, and thought.
- Aesthetic, social, and moral elevations are of enormous importance in mimetic art education.
- The student's media, object, and manner determine the construction of mimetic artwork.
- Art education has a more philosophical basis than history (Aristotle, 1984b, Book 9, p. 2323).
- We classify a poet, musician, dancer and painter not in relation to their mimetic representations but in relation to their media.
- The object of the mimetic art for Aristotle is to represent people as either good or bad, elevated or base, honourable or dishonourable, happy or unhappy, upright or depraved, lucky or unlucky, strong or weak, prosperous or poor, vile or delightful, spontaneous or cautious.
- Teaching children and adults to construct and recognise the object as so-and-so. Through recognition, imitation in art education can correspond to the knowledge of the things themselves. It is a process that is committed to and capable of seeking out the case for other kinds of recognitions.
- Mimesis can represent people in direct action, in third person, through narratives, speeches, verse, movement, and direct impersonation.
- Mimesis in art education can involve all manner of diverse language games, metre, melody, movement, or image construction. Our music teacher might ask the school's drama class to listen to the melody more closely when singing *Chitty Chitty Bang Bang*. The song, *Chitty Chitty Bang Bang* is an example of how words become lyrics that respond to and are given meaning by a musical performance with its own internal-external dependent reality.
- Mimesis aims at qualification and obligation. It is a process concerned with "what it is and that it is" (Aristotle, 1984, Book 6, p. 1619).
- The teaching of mimesis is couched in tradition, declarative and ascribing qualities, improvisation, invention, selectivity, spectacle, complete action, episodes, necessity, reality, imagination, revelation, and meaning.
- Mimesis is ingrained with the incidents of life.

- Aristotle argues that the imitative work of art in education can pronounce general truths (Aristotle, 1984b, Book 6, p. 2320). Issues that relate to what things are, about who we are, what we seem to be about, and what we would like things to be. The production knowledge of this imitation in art education can relate to universality when the student constructs the probable and necessary things we say and do: typically, normally and characteristically. The knowledge production must be shown to be perceptible, realistic, possible, credible, and reliable. Imitation in art education relates to whether an audience agrees that the mimetic artwork "communicates intelligible images of what it is reasonable" (Halliwell, 2002, p. 154) to suppose.
- If we want a guideline for teaching how art imitates with all the flexibility and security we require for education, then Aristotle supplies us with one: "The poet being an imitator just like the painter or other maker of likenesses, he must necessarily in all instances represent things... either as they were or are, or as they are said or thought to be or to have been, or as they ought to be" (Aristotle, 1984b, Book 25, p. 2337).
- Aristotle is attempting to demonstrate, above all, what is good about imitation in art education: "however small their capacity for it; the reason of the delight in seeing the picture is that one is at the same time learning—gathering the meaning of things, e.g. that the man there is so-and-so" (Aristotle, 1984b, Book 4, p. 2318).
- For Aristotle, the arts in mimetic ways in education make good use of how, in the right way, they can discover, devise, treat, express, and act with knowledge and consciousness (Aristotle, 1984b, Book 14, p. 2326).

III

Our sketch of some of the pedagogy and knowledge production issues relating to mimesis will assist us now to evaluate further Plato's and Aristotle's thinking of imitation in art education. We will contrast and compare their respective philosophy.

Plato scrutinises the relevance of art education as mimetic practice from at least three different but interrelated perspectives. The first perspective is his epistemological concern as to whether imitation in art education can demonstrate knowledge. His second perspective is whether ethically, mimesis as a teaching practice in art is good for children. The third perspective is how he explains what an imitator of art is.

Now, the basic epistemological question that Plato raises is whether art education is of the order of first, second, or third division knowledge. In Book Ten of *The Republic* he comes to the conclusion which was an argument that began in Book Two of *The Republic,* namely that art occupies third division knowledge production (Plato, 1997b, Book 10, p 1202). What does he mean by third division knowledge production? Plato is not only claiming that art education is of low knowledge output, he is also claiming positively that it has knowledge of a sort which, he maintains, does complete an education (Plato, 1997b, Book 3, p. 1040) and is essential for the love of it. This is what R.G. Collingwood in his 1925 paper *Philosophy of Art and Mind* discusses and what Alexander Nehamas generally agrees with, in his 1982 paper *Plato on Imitation and Poetry in Republic 10*. On the other hand, although art completes education, John Dewey argues in *Art as Experience* that art education for Plato is no more than a stepping stone: just the first rung on the ladder that children need to step on in order to progress in their development towards 'higher' knowledge of the world. "Art is to educate us away from art to perception of purely rational essences" (Dewey, 1980, p. 291). Dewey staunchly objects to this move on the grounds that it would be detrimental to a flourishing culture and human social relationships.

Dewey clearly recognised a flaw in Plato's argument. Can Plato reasonably show that art education never uses knowledge to enrich its experiences and connectedly that it lacks control over the actions and proper judgements that it exercises? According to Nehamas, Plato "believes that the painter lifts the surface off the subject and transplants it onto the painting" (Nehamas, 1982, p. 62). By thus analysing wrongly art in education as so construed, Plato's conclusion that art is third division knowledge is also incorrect, since it is based on the belief in part, 'that the painter lifts the surface off the subject and transplants it onto the painting'.

However misconceived Plato's construct of knowledge production of art education is, this does not get rid of his argument entirely. Plato can still ask, what value does art education have? An argument of this kind relates to the "ontological status of its appearance" (Gadamer, 1998, p. 13). As Gadamer underlines, Aristotle supplies an answer to this problem. What escapes Plato but not Aristotle (Aristotle, 1984b, Book 9, p. 2323), Dewey and Gadamer here, is how poetry imitates not history as an historian would write about, but "like the reality...in our sense of the term" (Aristotle, 1984b, Book 15, p. 2327). "The immediacy of the mode of poetic enactment is not required for the sake of a deceptive simulation of life, but in order to be the vehicle of a structure of meaning which Aristotle believes can nourish the understanding and move the emotions with ethical force" (Halliwell, 1998, p. 137). If art in education is 'like the reality...in our sense of the term', by writing, performing and drawing it, how Plato proceeds to class such art as bereft of truth "is a result of a mythology of what is accomplished by argument" (Diamond, 1996, p. 9).

Plato's theory of art education believes that, on the one hand, a student can learn to imitate things in nature and, on the other hand, that this process of learning does not require knowledge of the things themselves (Plato, 1997b, Book 10, p. 1201-3). Excellence in appearance is not the same epistemologically as excellence in conception which are always superior to appearances in art. Plato's theory is suggesting that images in art can be reflections of the things themselves without in essence being of the things themselves. So, a further reason why Plato construes art as having third division status connects to the fact that art education is interested in the look, feel, movement, image, and sound of things and shows a bias towards these things when constructing art. Yet, if we come back to Aristotle's argument that the production process of art education is attempting to reveal something to the senses of 'what it is and that it is', would we then be correct to assume that art education is imitating nothing more than the surface of things? Dewey (1980) notes that if we try to turn art into a philosophical reflection, we erase the manifestation of art as experienced. Direct and immediate sense qualitative experiences are then extinguished in order to adopt a standard concept which bears little resemblance to the artwork's actual vividness and meaning in experience. The relevance or lack of significance in art lies in the experience of it, not in philosophy *per se*. Furthermore, if art education is as fickle as Plato surmises, can this be sustained when mimetically the student constructs a likeness that purports to be a "realism which depends on the idea of an external relation between the logical characteristics of things and the logical features built into our modes of expression" (Diamond, 1996, p. 142)?

IV

One of Plato's propositions is that imitation in art education makes use of the concept of what a likeness is. Hence, as an example, for a student completing a painting, "[i]t is for the picture or some part of it, to be a pictorial likeness of an object of that sort" (Charlton, 2000, p. 473). A pictorial representation is neither a drama, musical or dance representation, and a pictorial likeness by itself still has to be filled out with what constitutes a 'good' resemblance and a 'bad' resemblance for a six-year-old and a fifteen-year-old. When our art examiner comes to the school and does not know the student's sitter in the painting, we might think that he or she cannot possibly know what the student has constructed as a likeness of the subject. However, our examiner will still be competent enough to know what succeeds as a likeness and they will study the student's evidence for this in a variety of ways. The student's sketchbook would demonstrate to the examiner how they are exploring the sitter's features and the corresponding resemblances between the images executed in the sketchbook and their final piece of work. The resemblance between the sitter and the picture of this sitter depends on its art and the teacher is encouraging the student, in this instance, to see the sitter representatively being evoked by their media, mark making skills and an openness towards the perceptual context of the appearance of the sitter.

Furthermore, what if the student is interested in a radically different kind of likeness of their sitter? What if the student starts off producing a likeness that begins as a duplicate model but then in the course of this exercise something happens by chance which transforms the artwork's images of the sitter? Should the student be ready to take seriously whatever they uncover when they draw to realise? What if slowly but surely the student brings the feeling of life into their painting so the likeness that is now created is very different from the one they started off with? What happens if the student sees something he or she did not see at first which makes them want to now change the study they have created? Plato, might still reply that these are just image making exercises but what if the student in such a process shows more vulnerability or sorrow of their model, or their stiffness, their seduction and beauty, their innocence and joy, the poverty of their lives, the sleepiness of the figure, a kindness about their sitter, their boredom or their quirky appearance? Perhaps it is the way the model clenches her fists awkwardly across her body that suggests to the student just the right kind of likeness the student is interested in exploring.

The imitation process, as Gadamer announces, is a showing one. Likeness is only as revealing as the thing is shown to be in art education. "For imitation enables us to see more than so-called reality. What is shown is, so to speak, elicited from the flux of manifold reality. Only what is shown is intended and nothing else" (Gadamer, 1998, p. 129). We must therefore see the likeness that the student has created by what their representation begets. If we judge the student's artwork merely by the 'pictorial likeness of an object of that sort, we will surely fail to appreciate what is being shown as a showing in itself.

The artist Jim Dine is, to some extent, noted for his imitations of nature but "Dine's interest in flower imagery emerged first in his prints because, he recalls, 'I saw in hard-ground etching the way to be precise in rendering the flowers that came from these steel engravings'. When making prints for some years afterwards, it seemed natural to Dine to work not from life but from other prints, in which the forms had already been translated into line" (Livingstone, 1994, p. 11). Dine's mimetic representations are not only taken from engraving techniques but also from the flower imagery in the engravings, from different flower imagery in general, from the physical marks his actions make, from his observational, imaginative and emotional responses to his ongoing artwork, from his reshaping of forms on the surface of the paper and from his understanding of botanical illustrations. Dine sees himself as a romantic artist and the medium he uses corresponds to what he genuinely feels about flowers and nature, from the qualities of his representation, from what he understands about structure, historical associations, composition, chance, colour relationships, metaphor, symbolism, lighting, texture and tones, and from prior experiences. Hence, his creation of a flower likeness is the result of many complex, unifying, and interrelated responses.

Substituting Jim Dine for a student in our class or studio working from a set of flowers is to beg the question how the student is first observing the flowers: on a table in the centre of a room, against a window or French doors, or in a corner space surrounded by a few other objects and are the flowers in some sort of plant pot or are they placed on the table as they are? Why do people put them on graves and why do they wear them in their hair and around their necks, why are they sent to people with messages attached? What are they for? Other questions are: Has the student created a likeness that sensibly involves an abstract order sophisticated enough to consolidate the figurative presence of it brevity? Are there botanical, naturalistic or scientific characteristics about the artwork or does it appear like a romantic-idealist or minimalist piece of stylistic intent? Perhaps the student adopts a likeness similar to Georgia O'Keeffe's or Emil Nolde's flower paintings. They may even want to create a photomontage in the political style of John Heartfield of their flowers, or as a sign of peace? Do the flowers lend themselves to all these possible interpretations without sacrificing what the flowers exhibit? In its likeness does the student's artwork make public, as Heidegger (2000, p. 145) discerns, something other than the mere thing itself, a flower?

The artist William Hogarth was noted for his moral satire on life in his 1731 *Harlot's Progress* and in his 1742-4 *A Rake's Progress*. In both works he wanted his artwork to appear like a theatrical representation, a stage drama. Dario Fo's *Accidental Death Of An Anarchist* was first performed on stage in 1970, William Blake's *Newton* (1795), and Richard Hamilton, John McHale and John Voelcker's (1956) *Just What Is It That Makes Today's Homes So Different, So Appealing?* These are all artworks that would have displeased Plato because they demonstrate a multitude of ways that display how art mimetically can "mix together and separate" (Plato, 1997a, p. 363). The frightening thing for art education is that Plato (1997b, Book 3, p. 1032) would have then rejected William Blake for his poetry and fine art mixing and for his satire of Newton; he would have rejected Dario Fo's play for his loose portrait of the facts of the case and his reliance on comedy, and he would have rejected William Hogarth for the mixing of theatrical drama with fine art. While Dario Fo's *Accidental Death Of An Anarchist* is fictional, the play keeps the audience always in the possible, demonstrating as it does "a particular point" (Aristotle, 1984b, Book 6, p. 2320). Plato clearly wanted to see a 'pure' and plain style applied to the teaching of mimetic art, believing that this was the best way to integrate young people into society (Plato, 1997b, Book 3, p. 1034–5).

Plato would have appreciated at one level *Just What Is It That Makes Today's Homes So Different, So Appealing?* Nevertheless, in this artwork the image-making appearance would have disturbed him, the likeness of which he would never have approved of because of its alleged lack in appearance of sufficient knowledge (Plato, 1997b, Book 10, p. 1203). We can question this retort again from him as we have done via Aristotle's indispensable argument relating to the concept of recognition. Everything in this mixed-media artwork "involves making delicate discriminations and discerning subtle relationships, identifying symbol systems and characters within these systems and what these characters denote and exemplify, interpreting works and reorganising the world in terms of works and in terms of the world" (Goodman, 1986, p. 191).

To be sure, *Just What Is It That Makes Today's Homes So Different, So Appealing?* Reflects the artists' self-understanding but, it is still a self-understanding full of actual knowledge of the world whose images allegorically remain as true to life events. One could reply that this is a little unfair of us because such art did not exist like this in Plato's time. Maybe we should think, as Aristotle did, that Homer, Euripides, Sophocles, and Aristophanes were poets whose faults could be rationalised in such a way that "if the poet's description be criticised as not true to fact, one may urge perhaps that the object ought to be as described—an answer like that of Sophocles, who said that he drew men as they ought to be, and Euripides as they are. If the description, however, be neither true nor of the thing as it ought to be, the answer must be then, that it is in accordance with opinion" (Aristotle, 1984b, Book 25, p. 2338). As a further teaching issue, what attitude should the teacher take when, as Aristotle mentions, the child shows a technical error in their performance or representation that is "only accidentally connected with the poetic art" (Aristotle, 1984b, Book 25, p. 2338)?

In making the appearance of a bed, the artist, for Plato, has to handle all those things that make it a particular appearance of it. An adequate appreciation of a bed in appearance is not seen as equal to an adequate appreciation of the concept of it. A student may have an eloquent style of writing but have no idea of what makes it eloquent. For example, a student may be capable of a 'perfect' match of one of Casper David Friedrich's landscape paintings. In creating an 'exact' likeness, however, it does not follow that the student understands the ideas behind Friedrich's work and if they do not understand these ideas, of what consequence is the imitation (Cannatella, 2004, p. 69)? We can paint a man or woman a million times and in a million different ways and still not know anything necessarily more about him or her, if all we are doing is executing appearances arbitrarily. Sustained familiarity and realisation, not uninformed actions, are what the teacher encourages in imitation in art. Mimetic teaching requires from the student that they are touched by questions and actions of their own making whose depth of insight is discernible. To remove any random performance and misrepresentation, the students learn to develop control over their subject-matter by restricting themselves to the task in hand. They take care not to separate their perceptions from the spirit of the thing and from a point where there is intensity in their actions. This means that the unveiling of recognition in art teaching has a relation to the fact that the "wholeness of an image is not an outlying wholeness produced by its contents, but an in-dwelling wholeness thoroughly pervading its content and indistinguishable from them" (Todes, 2001, p. 145).

If each student painting captures a different life of our individual through appearances, are we not compelled to think that each painting exists as a knowing different painting? The photographer Arnold Newman in his photographs of Pier Mondrian in 1942, Max Ernst in 1942, Igor Stravinsky in 1946 and Pablo Picasso in 1954 are elevated examples of an art that require from us an understanding of each picture quality, that Newman clearly understands his subjects and connectedly why we must see the allegorical nature of each works symbolic content. His 1963 photograph of the industrial magnate Alfried Krupp who was convicted at the Nuremberg trials of war crimes is the kind of deep likeness making that Plato never comes to grips with but Aristotle does in his *Poetics*. Aristotle recognised the coping skills of the artist to know why he needed to create a staged artifice of a man visible but unseen, the process which affects the construction of this story and the enunciating power of its attraction.

"The content of 'mind' is not only thought; sensual experience is as much mental as intellectual reflection" (Graham, 1995, p. 32). In which case, the student in their represented painting of a bed may be demonstrating aesthetically something more than what a bed is theoretically, just as the artist Tracy Emin in her *My Bed* (1998) work, is more than a mattress, linen and four pillows. "John Burger once demonstrated, we can see caught in Gainsborough's portrait of the Andrews, something that they themselves may not have been able to see, a distinctively proprietarily attitude" (Graham, 1995).

How accurate can art education be if art education encourages, as Collingwood declares, "an orgy of misrule" (Collingwood, 1925, p. 156)? Can it produce 'what it is and that it is' if the education of art is 'an orgy of misrule? Is everything we have said so far worthless now? What Collingwood is referring to is how our passions and affections play an important role in the creation of art that Plato hitherto had noted. When the student is creating art they do so argues Plato, in rhythmical, sensuous, instinctive, pleasurable, melodic, visionary and kinetic ways. There is a "constant search for novelty" (Plato, 1997, p. 1348). By working in this way "the artist does not have an adequate grasp of the functional specifications, and thus of a vital part of the nature, of the objects that he represents. This is the main reason why Plato objects to the artist's lack of concern with the 'invisible' or nonsensible" (Moravcsik, 1982, p. 38). This is puzzling because, surely, as an example, Arnold Newman's photograph of Alfried Krupp (1962) does just that; it exposes the invisible through visual means: "it makes visible that which one should not be able to see and which one is not able to see without astonishment" (Marion, 2004, p. 1). The unseen is uncovered and rendered in Newman's photograph. Picasso's *Guernica* (1937), Charles Dickens' *Nicholas Nickleby*, Franz Kafka's *The Trial*, Jane Austen's *Pride and Prejudice*, or Mary Oliver's *Wild Geese*, show in different modes how the arts confront us with the invisible and expose it. Furthermore, we should not get carried away with art education being 'an orgy of misrule', as this implies that art education is undisciplined and flimsy. To reiterate, teaching mimetically is concerned with how students are actualising the possibilities of recognition, a way of revealing something 'as', and to think otherwise is nonsense.

Yes, Plato sees art as an "imitation of appearance," (Plato, 1997b, Book 10, p. 1202) but he derives this grip to be "easily produced without knowledge of the truth" (Plato, 1997b, Book 10, p. 1203). But again what kind of truth are we talking about? And few art lessons, if any, ignore what is essential to recognise, know, and learn. What is reached for in performance or represented in an art lesson is precisely the refined that defies us and provokes us. If we were to accept Collingwood's notion that art education presupposes 'an orgy of misrule' as a main stay of art education we would be seriously risking what we have said all along about imitation in art education; namely, that children in an art lesson will deposit meaning through recognition. The "aesthetic of non-differentiation" (Gadamer, 1989, p. 117) is opposed, because it is not an education that recognises what the musician is playing, the dancer is choreographing; and the process whereby our student makes his poem stand out telling us something about the real experience of life that is no accident of construction. We can reject Plato's theory of art because the concept of imitation as recognition is missing. Recognition in art education does not come from a "dark affair" (Plato, 1997b, Book X, p. 1201) a mystical production. Rather, "every representation finds its genuine fulfilment simply in the fact that what it represents is emphatically there" (Gadamer, 1998, p. 119). There is real life going on and living growth from the child in the art class or studio but Plato is constantly telling us that that art is only images, "not things that are" (Plato, 1997b, Book X, p. 1203). Ignoring the sense of life in the child's art is to exclude the child's vision of life, and "no matter how much the variety of the performance or the realisation of such a structure can be traced back to the conception of the players—it also does not remain in the subjectivity of what we think, but it is embodied there. Thus it is not at all a question of a mere subjective variety of conceptions, but of the work's own possibilities of being that emerge as the work explicates itself, as it were, in the variety of its aspects" (Gadamer, 1989, p. 117–8).

V

We have stated briefly how Plato misjudges art education mimetically but we have yet to examine his view on how art education teaching should be taught. What kind of mimetic material should the teacher teach in art? To answer this question is to state that the only imitation that is to be allowed in art education is when it helps to form good habits. The student should imitate people who are virtuous: "courageous, self-controlled and pious" (Plato, 1997b, Book 3, p. 1033). This is not the kind of programme that I have painted in Section One of this chapter. Courage, self-control and piousness, however well intentioned these virtues are, do not make a syllabus and they do not explain syntactically how the knowledge production of mimesis in art education is to embody them. As indisputably good a person we want the student to be, being a good person in the Platonic sense implied will not establish how the student is to play the cello well. The student has to be musically trained to play the cello well.

Aristotle agrees with Plato that students should be acting virtuously when singing, dancing, or when writing poems and stories. However, he does not quite go along with this either, because he argues that the "character in a play is that which reveals the choice of the agents" (Aristotle, 1984b, Book 6, p. 2321). Characters have to be real even if the student is acting out the role of a malicious character in a play. Tragedy should be constructed to arouse pity and fear (Aristotle, 1984b, Book 6, p. 2321) and "a good poet often stretches out a plot beyond its capabilities, and is thus obliged to twist the sequence of an incident" (Aristotle, 1984b, Book 9, p. 2323). The student with all the righteous virtues in the world must still restore to art its real presentation and the "obligatoriness" (Gadamer, 1989, p. 118) of thoughts and actions expressive of art.

Plato asks: "don't you understand that we first tell stories to children?" (Plato, 1997b, Book 2, p. 1015). He unequivocally wants to protect children and to make sure they are safe, the state must create laws. The knowable world is to be censured from above. Plato rejects poetry, particularly staged performances, for their lack of understanding of what constitutes the good. Yet the overcoming of circumstantiality and ignorance that Plato clearly wants to see cannot be effective by censuring means alone. Undoubtedly related to this as Plato explicates is the notion that philosophy and poetry have long had an adversarial relationship: 'let's also tell poetry that there is an ancient quarrel between it and philosophy'. The quarrel is about the precision of philosophy versus the reputed discursive thinking of poetry which, for Plato, is all too often misleading. Plato makes a serious point. But is philosophical thinking inexorably more right and more accurate than poetic thinking about the world? While "[a] general account may give us necessary conditions for choosing well; it cannot by itself give sufficient conditions" (Nussbaum, 1992, p. 93). I want to quote some short passages from Frederick Schiller because he shows to us what poetry can bring as useful to this situation. "Man, neither altogether satisfied with the senses, nor forever capable of thought, wanted a middle state, a bridge between the two states, bringing them into harmony" (Schiller, 2006 p. 240). "Law only governs the actions" (Schiller, 2006, p. 240). "Where the influence of civil laws ends, that of the stage begins" (Schiller, 2006, p. 240). Whereas, poetry is partly responsible for controlling "the heart and follows thought to the source" (Schiller, 2006, p. 240). "Where venality and corruption blind and bias justice and judgement, and intimidation perverts its ends, the stage seizes the sword and scales and pronounces a terrible verdict on vice" (Schiller, 2006, p. 240). "When morality is no more taught, religion no longer received, or laws exist, Medea would still terrify us with her infanticide. The sight of Lady Macbeth, while it makes us shudder, will also make us rejoice in a good conscience, when we see her, the sleep-walker, washing her hands and seeking to destroy the awful smell of murder. Sight is always more powerful to man than description; hence the stage acts more powerfully than morality or law" (Schiller, 2006, p. 240). "But in this the stage only aids justice. A far wider field is really open to it. There are a thousand vices unnoticed by human justice, but condemned by the stage; so, also, a thousand virtues overlooked by man's law are honoured on the stage" (Schiller, 2006, p. 240). "Vice is portrayed on the stage in an equally telling manner. Thus, when old Lear, blind, helpless…is seen knocking in vain at his daughters' doors, and in tempest and night he recounts by telling his woes to the elements, and ends by saying: 'I have given you all',—how strongly impressed we feel at the value of filial piety, and how hateful ingratitude seems to us!" (Schiller, 2006, p. 241).

In the examples just shown, art education is constantly getting involved in the affairs of life which shift the narratives view points to emphasise, penetrate, and express some of the true realities of living. We find further in many children stories big bad wolves, monsters, ghouls, robots; murders, depravity, deceitfulness, wizards, witches, magic and talking bears. Plato had difficulty with such image-making stories. He objected to someone in a pantomime imitating trumpets, pulleys, dogs and cuckoos, "neighing horses, bellowing bulls, roaring rivers, the crashing sea, and thunder" (Plato, 1997b, Book 3, p. 1033-4). He never comes to grips with the benevolent fantasy of the child and their imaginative intelligence without which things can very quickly backfire on education to shackle the living lives of children, their ability to self-interrogate, recognise, and experience the measure of things for themselves, tell apart one thing from another and how things can make sense to them even if that thing is a talking bear.

"—I've got you—said the wolf, and yawned. The sheep turned its teary eyes toward him.—Do you have to eat me? Is it really necessary?

—Unfortunately, I must. This is how it happens in all the fables: Once upon a time a naughty sheep left its mother. In the forest it met a bad wolf who…" (Herbert, 1999, p. 65).

An aspect of Plato's position in *The Republic* is that the young can be easily fooled about the good life and seduced by it. In defence of Plato, Simon Blackburn admits that the written text, as much as the performance or image, may be "easily turned into an object of recitation or fetish, the foodstuff of unintelligent fundamentalism" (Blackburn, 2007, p. 6). Yet does the 'foodstuff of unintelligent fundamentalism' come from reading and appreciating *Winnie-the Pooh* or *The Day I Swapped My Dad For Two Goldfish*? In these two stories the children may find ways which freely and directly move them into the direction to do what is good.

As in Book Ten of *The Republic* Plato asserts that imitation in art education reproduces what comes easiest. As a teacher our reply might be that if a student imitated in this fashion, how convincing would the imitation be? How would they be able to piece together and preserve in their artwork some of the high dignity, tension and beauty of life? This still leaves the question whether art can be used for the purposes of 'unintelligent fundamentalism', but surely the same could be said for science, business, philosophy, or politics. Really, are we to think that the design and the building process that went into the Pantheon were easy? If we take a good look at any Greek sculpture from around the fourth century B.C. and observe their muscle structures, the position of humps and hollows in the bodies, their posture, proportions and gestures, are we to think that the artist reproduces what comes easiest? Our rebuttal is that imitation in art education is not easy to produce creatively. Ultimately, nothing can protect us from someone who is determined to use art or science for propaganda purposes. Making the artwork's recognition clear is surely a step to foil the 'foodstuff of unintelligent fundamentalism'? Plato has a point when he states: "The young can't distinguish what is allegorical from what isn't, and the opinions at this age are hard to erase and apt to become unalterable" (Plato, 1997b, Book II, p. 1017). However, the teaching of imitation in art is concerned, as we have noted, with distinguishing what is allegorical from what is not allegorical.

In the final analysis the value of art education, for Plato, is not whether the student sings or dances beautifully, but whether what is sung or danced is good (Plato, 1997, p. 1345–6) for society. The singing and dancing may be beautifully performed and thus good in this sense. However, his point is that some moral agreement is needed to distinguish what is good over and above what is visually or musically good as a performance. For example, "a work of art may be judged to be aesthetically good insofar as it is beautiful, is formally unified and strongly expressive, but aesthetically bad insofar as it trivialises the issues with which it deals and manifests ethically reprehensible attitudes" (Gaut, 2001, p. 183). Any student's artwork which attempted to display ethically reprehensible attitudes would be hard to accept educationally as a good work. However, a piece of music or a dance 'judged to be aesthetically good insofar as it is beautiful' may be morally good for us too. As Compte-Sponville maintains, we "would be less beautiful, less cultured, less happy …less true and less human" (Comte-Sponville, 2005, p. 108), if art education did not teach us the kind of contact that is needed to shape, see, feel, challenge, liberate, extend, respond, celebrate, and take pleasure from life.

Some theorists have argued that any abstract concept of what makes an actual artwork good is a long way short of judging the actual artwork of the student. Can a student's work of art also be a good work of art when "it takes a representative of the art-world to make a work of art" (Wollheim, 1998, p. 14)? If without seeing the student's artwork we have already determined what the good in their painting should be, then this is no more than an obscure account of "paintingness" (Wollheim, 1998, p. 15). Arthur Danto remarks whether we can "elicit equivalent experiences through inequivalent stimuli" (Danto, 1994, p. 150)? As Danto goes on to say in relation to Bishop Berkeley's theory of mind, "what the mind contains are ideas, and ideas are just their contents, so the difference between a cow and the idea of a cow is not there to be drawn by Berkeley, who is after all eager to identify cows with the idea of cows" (Danto, 1994, p. 151). "Thus the medium is a kind of metaphysical effigy for consciousness, in that it is never part of the picture but sacrifices itself as it were, in an act of total withdrawal and self-effacement, leaving only content" (Danto, 1994, p. 152).

The questionable status of the knowledge production which Plato attributes to art education is summed up by three questions Plato poses: "What does painting do in each case? Does it imitate that which is as it is, or does it imitate that which appears as it appears? Is it an imitation of appearance or of truth?" (Plato, 1997b, Book 10, p. 1202). Emphatically, Blackburn discredits this commentary. "The disastrous move here is to suppose that representing how something, such as a bed or a chair, or President Bush, appears, is not representing a bed or a chair or President Bush at all, but only this different thing, their appearance" (Blackburn, 2007, p. 151). As Blackburn continues, "for it does not seem to have occurred to Plato that representations may bring out new aspects of the very things they represent. The sundial or watch does not have to substitute for an interest in the time. A cartoon of your favourite politician does not just present a substitute or shadow to look at instead of the very person. It presents the person, looking perhaps mad, or bad, or wild or stupid, and thereby suggests, and potentially reveals, an aspect of the person" (Blackburn, 2007, p. 151–2).

VI

Nehamas interprets Plato as saying that "many make fun of me…but none of the unwise can act like me" (Nehamas, 1982, p. 57). We can make a number of distinctions from this. One is to do with how we can, in an uneducated manner, make fun of someone mimetically. Plato thinks, as shown in the above Nehamas quote, that it does not take a lot of intelligence in order for someone to physically mimic him. The bully in the class might mimic someone in a physical and vocal way. Plato, however, is making the distinction that in order to mimic him none of the unwise possess the talent to act like him. By this, he is indicating how difficult it is to imitate Plato's intellectual powers. One cannot act like him, claims Plato, unless one shows the philosophical nature of his thinking. The only way to imitate Plato would be to rationalise as he does. To mimic Plato, as he sees himself, is to think logically and wisely.

When our well rehearsed student actor comes on stage to orate from Shakespeare's *King Richard the Third*: "Now is the winter of our discontent made glorious summer by this sun of York; And all the clouds that lour'd upon our house" we know what the audience back then and the audience now are recognising in this soliloquy. This is Richard Duke of Gloucester and "knowledge here means recognition" (Gadamer, 1998, p. 119). We should distinguish between mimicking another person and making fun of ourselves. For example, our student-actor imitates Richard Duke of Gloucester in Shakespeare's *King Richard the Third*. In the text, Richard not only makes fun of himself but he is also very clever and devious. He describes how he sees himself and in so doing he exposes the essence of himself that we think of as representative of the man. Shakespeare speaks the language of poetry and identifies for us the character of Richard in Act One of the play:

"But I—that am not shap'd for sportive tricks,
Nor made to court an amorous looking glass—
I—that am rudely stamp'd, and want love's majesty
I—that am curtail'd of this fair proportion,
Cheated of features by dissembling nature,
Deform'd, unfinish'd sent before my time
Into this breathing world scarce half made up,
And that so lamely and unfashionable
That dogs bark at me as I halt by them"

The student-actor who plays the fool in a play is acting like the character he or she is supposed to be. Physical mimicking is different from verbal mimicking but in Shakespeare's *King Richard the Third* the mimicking we see by Richard is self-mocking and cunning. What shrug of the shoulders, facial expression, hand gesture or turning of the body is our student-actor deploying in his physical mimicry of Richard? Yet, Plato's point is surely that the unwise cannot behave like me, a remark that reinstates the importance that not any kind of mimicking will do and no teacher of drama would disagree with that. To mimic Plato on stage we would have to show the considerable intellectual talents he possessed.

The student-actor uses mime as a means to an end. He will not be content with just repeating the lines of Shakespeare's *Hamlet*; he will also want to be seen as Hamlet on stage, expressing what evokes the pain of Hamlet so as to produce a realistic performance of Shakespeare's character Hamlet. The tone, the gesture, the readiness, and the valedictory speeches have to be spoken with penetrating insight. Acting helps the audience to see more than the "dog that looks at the pointing hand" (Gadamer, 1998, p. 128).

Admittedly, what Plato is worried about in the broader sense is that a student could recite word-for-word one of his dialogues without really getting to grip with the argument of the dialogue. Learning becomes equated with memorisation. What we have is an education which favours mirroring appearances rather than intellectual understanding. This is only true, of course, if this imitation is the only kind of learning that an art teacher instructs about mimesis. 'Learning your lines' relates to learning to speak your lines: on time, softly, gently and with elegance. Our student-actor must know how to play their part with a performance the audience can recognise evocatively. Reciting a poem word-for-word may be seen as more than a test of memory, as it may generate the feeling that one is holding on to something important to remember. Other complications can arise if we have only a simple educational notion of mimicking. There is plenty of imitative work that goes on in dance and music performances but dance and music imitation teaching stresses not imitation in appearance but imitation in depth. Various mimetic stylistic turns and interpretations may be involved, for example, when playing the notes as instructed and when playing the notes as Purcell's piece (Davies, 2005, p. 499). As we have argued, it is proper for art education to be concerned with productive procedures. Stephen Halliwell mentions that these productive procedures are not the confines of literal copying which "condemns its products to the realm of the derivative and spurious" (Halliwell, 2002, p. 55). Indeed, Ernst Gombrich reminds us that an artist "cannot transcribe what he sees; he can only translate it into the terms of his medium" (Gombrich, 1977, p. 30) and "[t]he artist cannot copy a sunlit lawn, but he can suggest it" (Gombrich, 1977, p. 33).

From the above Nehamas quote, 'many make fun of me...but none of the unwise can act like me', we can further draw the conclusion that there is a difference between mimicking and emulation. One can mimic and emulate at the same time, just as a student can mimic and emulate his big brother or sister. Plato does not believe that a child should be given a free hand to mimic what they like. Imitation must comprehend "correctness" (Plato, 1997, p. 1348). Correctness for Plato would mean that the student shows himself to be Plato's equal or has shown himself to understand the passage. But equally, we have to note from Aristotle that "the art imitating by means of the action on the stage" (Aristotle, 1984b, Book 22, p. 2335) involves another kind of correctness. At one level what Aristotle is driving at in his *Poetics* is not straightforwardly a mimicking and emulating task; it is an *art*. The performance demands an art that is familiar, veracious, and moving. Because it is an art we are talking about, our students must proceed by their own experiences and that of others familiar with the art form.

Plato wants educational imitation to convey good people, good rules, and good situations, (Nehamas, 1982, p. 49) in life, on stage, as well as in novels. He overlooks the extent to which this requires an art in life, on stage, and in novels. Drama as tragedy is not just a report of what has happened, stating the facts of the case. The performance needs exemplary moments of acting, of deliberate voice inflexions, humane munificence, and 'masterful' images of tenderness, suffering, resistance, provocation, remorse, and tyranny, if the audience in the theatre is to believe that such a person is good or bad. Acting must have a hold upon the audience's attention, saturating their senses. Stage production must engage the audience. Aristotle states that educationally, when the student acts on stage, the imitative part they play should involve those incidents that arouse the conveying of goodness and badness (Aristotle, 1984b, Book 9, p. 2323). This arousing, designed to produce an emotional and thoughtful response, Aristotle sees as a necessary aspect of the craft characterising enactment. What arouses the audience is what will open them up to the good and the bad situation in the drama as truth-to-life. The student's art in a play is imitating true-to-life incidents which, Aristotle proposes, requires perceptions of reality as much as knowing intellectually. The poet's art is significant in itself. In this case, the student's art relates to testing ideas in their own acute manner and with the constraints of what is literally present in the obvious and subtle formalities of what constitutes a good or bad person. We find that it is in this educational art which the teacher is often concerned about, an enactment which awakens the nature of the drama's reality. In a further twist away from Plato, Aristotle realises that the artist's art in terms of melody, tragedy, comedy and so forth, represents elements of difference in the arts, which Aristotle calls "means of their imitation" (Aristotle, 1984b, Book 1, p. 2316–7). The imitation has moved on from being only a factor of what a good person is to being also an art of imitation. A factor of this art is how the art's productive procedure creates a melody, plot, story, metaphor, rhyme, and sonnet. The student's art-producing procedure influences the results of their musicological scholarship. Knowing how comedy is performed is having knowledge of the art of it. It is this imitational practice, Aristotle surmises, that sets art education apart.

It is only when "states arise out of like activities" (Aristotle, 1984a, Book II, p. 1743) that the good is seen. Knowing the like activity is evident when the student-actor performs it 'like this', 'can you do this' and 'do you recognise this' as like activities that contribute to excellence in art education. Now, perform it 'like this' may seem to vindicate Plato's argument of 'putting knowledge into souls' but the paradox is that art education cannot be putting knowledge into souls "since they are only images, not things that are" (Plato, 1997b, Book 10, p. 1203). We have seen how Blackburn defeats that argument.

The teacher can say what the performance needs is 'like this' but the way you are performing it is not "like this"; 'can you see the difference'? Aristotle surely convinces us, "it is from playing the lyre that both good and bad lyre-players are produced" (Aristotle, 1984a, Book II, p. 1743). The differences between the good and the bad playing are in the doing, where, for Aristotle, the good arises out of lyre-player's mimetic activities. When you can produce artwork mimetically in painting, sculpture, acting, cinematography, writing, architecture, and singing, for example, the appropriate form of the good in one sense, is grasped by the student. As previously remarked, 'like this' in art education presupposes a showing, and the showing is an indispensable attempt to express significance in its own right.

Imitation in art education is: (1) a natural impulse of life, (2) a part of a realistic attitude to learning, (3) it embraces truth to life experiences, (4) it's an effective and efficient form of learning, (5) it concerns familiarity and recognition, (6) it stimulates excitement because it is of this world, (7) it is a precise, supple and creative form of intelligence in art education, (8) it is a part of a process that corresponds to learning that gathers the meaning and showing of a plethora of things, (9) knowledge production is an important part of it, and (10) it expresses 'what it is and that it is' as an art.

In Section One of this chapter I outlined an agenda concerned with the teaching of mimesis in art education. This was followed by an analysis of Plato's and Aristotle's understanding of mimesis in art education. We have ascertained how, on the one hand, Plato insists that the imitative work of art in education is "inferior in respect to truth" (Plato, 1997b, Book 10, p. 1209), and on the other hand, we have seen Aristotle insist, contrary to Plato, that the imitative work of art in education can pronounce general truths (Aristotle, 1984b, Book 6, p. 2320). Our educational discussion has focused on some of the intricacies of Plato and Aristotle. We have been open to Plato's criticism of art education, but our reply has been that generally he misconstrues the mimetic art educational process in conceptual and perceptive ways. Without a doubt, he shows himself to have a very limited understanding of the complexity and meaning of art education. His empirical evidence is poor. In contrast, Aristotle's *Poetics* explains many of the characteristics of mimetic art education. He shows himself in his *Poetics* to be a much better analytical philosopher of art education than Plato. While the demonstration of an argument is perhaps stronger in Plato than Aristotle, Plato's deduction that art education is thrice removed from the truth is a statement unsupportable by the facts as we have discussed them here.

Subsequently, in this first chapter we have explored extensively the mimetic production of educational knowledge. The elegance of it and what can be good about imitation in art education has been discussed, along with the capabilities that are sometimes needed for it. We have seen how mimesis in art education is a changing and 'intentional historical characterisation of art-making'. With the teaching of children in mind, we have further outlined the importance imitation has for learning, and its life-serving significance. Our discourse throughout has shown how to stimulate the essential notion of mimesis which is recognition and how in turn recognition can be constructed in meaningful diverse situations. At length we have examined ways to teach mimesis expansively and thoughtfully. Differences have been discussed between the representative and enacting attributes of mimesis. In a practical manner we have demonstrated how children can mimetically create art. Educationally, it is the children's own sensitivity and outlook that must be engaged and supported, but through a process which helps them to identify, realise, and develop representation-enactment qualities in their constructions. What the child configures mimetically, we all can recognise as derivative and exemplary of real life whether that be in a story about robots, otters or happiness. Mimesis is an extant and thriving practice. I believe that there is every reason why we should be proud of mimetic production in art education, as it is not only natural and pleasurable for the child. It is also common in life and seems to be indisputably adroit, proper and essential for ruling on some of the things in this world that are true of it.

ART AS EXPERIENCE

John Dewey

"The aesthetic is a way of articulating experience" (Alexander, 1987, p. 250).

Abstract

Discerning from the beginning to its end, Art as Experience is still one of the most comprehensive thesis for art educators and policy makers alike. Testing, questioning, and tough, it examines what embodies a thriving and healthy society, and argues that art education is essential to such conditions. Dewey claims correctly that art education can never be a literal experience, a leveller, a rule, a matter of reason alone or a moral function and cannot be governed by charts, bureaucracy, conventionality, and statistics. For education this has major consequences about how art should be taught. Dewey is adamant: art is in the lead in what constitutes new vision. To be able to pluck the benefits of this art for our social system of education, Dewey maintains, as this chapter will explore, that art teaching must revolve around what Art as Experience evokes in its nature.

Introduction

Dewey was seventy-five when he wrote *Art as Experience* in 1934 (Jackson, 1998, p. xi). The aim of this chapter is to give an interpretation, albeit a partial one, of this outstanding work. I will discuss how Dewey underlines art education with its own connecting importance. He is unyielding, however, that art education does not just happen; it has to be harnessed and taught, where "in the very substance of art" (Dewey, 1980, p. 212) it reverberates with the hustle and bustle, expansion and renewal, tempo and industry of the present in experience.

A programme of education for Dewey must be conducive to students' capabilities, interests and accumulated handling of their past experiences, open to and realisable in a social environment which nurtures a "wider and better balanced environment than that by which the young would be likely, if left to themselves to be influenced" (Dewey, 1944, p. 22). It is prudent to say that his position, as much in evidence in his *Democracy and Education,* theorises a democratic social constructive process that is compatible with the student's free capacity to enjoy, act, and think intelligibly. An educational environment where the student develops their experience of living together with others, taking an active part in educational opportunities, influencing events, and strengthening commitments all within the certainty that their experiences matter. This last point, that student experiences matter, has an all important place in *Art as Experience*.

To meet these challenges Dewey wants to underpin the arts in education with a "pragmatic pedagogy" (Biestra, 1995, p. 105) that motivates and galvanises. A social democratic educational environment for Dewey that includes art education is a pulsating, cooperative, coordinating, and modified process in harmony with the world around it (Dewey, 1944, p. 10-22). Dewey believes that art education reflects the wider and fuller expansion of individual and community sympathies and values. Relying on recognised and well respected historical and current examples at the time when he was writing *Art as Experience*, he attempts to explain how art excels in human becoming to stimulate and expand our lives. We have to ask that if art education is as germane as he claims it to be, he must demonstrate its public service. How does he do this?

Let us note that in *Art as Experience* Dewey has a number of intentions. Firstly, he confronts what prevents art as experience. This point is sometimes overlooked by theorists, policy makers, politicians, and teachers. Why should we see this as an issue not to be overlooked? There are reasons for us to discuss this, not least because Dewey perceives it as a disconcerting problem for art in education. Secondly, he wants to demonstrate that the course of art in education should be continuous with natural impulses, community values, and everyday experiences which influence the students' artwork and our environment in a variety of ways. Thirdly, he wants to show some of the processes of art production and execution and fourthly, why art as experience is valuable for a democratic social life and education. Dewey propounds that our ordinary experiences strengthen the teaching of art, manifesting some of our more cherished social actions and sympathies. Ordinary experiences are derivative of common feelings that can prompt the reshaping and protection of one's environment. Art in education is to communicate the character of our everyday experiences in the world with resonance and reverberation.

This chapter is broken down into two sections. First, I will discuss what impedes art as an experience for Dewey. Second, I will discuss what Dewey means by experience in art, and concordantly why natural impulses, culture, the environment and everyday experiences must act as dominant centripetal fields in art education.

I

Barriers which can Obstruct Art as an Experience

Dewey does not agree that morality can be the sole rule-giving ground for art education. This is not without precedent. Aristotle in his *Poetics* writes that "there is not the same kind of correctness in poetry as in politics, or indeed in any other art" (Aristotle, 1984, Book 25, p. 2337). The grandfather of Western philosophy, Plato, never pretended that art could function as a model of morality, for the obvious reason that art dispenses the particular and not the universal. In Book Ten of *The Republic* he implies that some art always has a particular place, event, person, colour, or theme it has in mind when it tackles the appearance of an 'object'. A student has a particular bed design they want to make as a model or in a short story they have written they describe a particular person in some detail. Teaching art involves quintessentially how the artwork looks and how it is being performed. Our student gains local knowledge of their 'object' by forming impressions of it that oscillates with its mode of production. Dealing only with the way the student supposedly creates an image of their object and its effects and the further fact that appearances can be variable may manifest "ethically reprehensible attitudes" (Gaut, 2001, p. 183).

To implement unmitigated moralising pressure upon art education suggests to Dewey that it can "miss a sense of the way in which art exercises its human function" (Dewey, 1980, p. 346). One of the ways this can happen is when we "treat works of art as a kind of sublimated Aesop's fables" (Dewey, 1980, p. 346). Art education becomes bound to a clear case of moral obligation. We could then endorse a programme of art teaching that rests less on art as "receptive to the image at the moment it appears" (Bachelard, 1994, p.xiv), and more on whether the art experience is being guided by a fundamental principle of moral conduct. In a reference to Shakespeare's plays, Dewey notes how a conventional morality can be "ingeniously extracted" (Dewey, 1980, p. 349) from it and, then, perhaps act as an account of it. The premise being that however dramatic the art is, didactically the work's representation is turned into a scene for moral communication. This is its value. Our attention to Shakespeare can become satisfied by an indubitable conventional morality that regulates our judgements about the recognition of art. If moral standing overrides all aesthetic experiences "our eyes have been reduced to instruments with which to identify and to measure; hence we suffer a paucity of ideas that can be expressed in images and an incapacity to discover meaning in what we see" (Arnheim, 1974, p. 1).

The reality of life portrayed in art through the centuries has at times enraged the public. Was the Inquisition in the Counter-Reformation correct to demand from the Renaissance painter Paolo Veronese that he must remove the drunken figures and Germans in his painting the *Wedding of Cana* (1562-3)? Edouard Manet's painting, *Olympia* (1863), or D.H. Lawrence's novel, *Lady Chatterley's Lover,* were in the past mocked as depraved works of art.

In Shakespeare's *The Tempest*, Ariel returns singing:

"Where the bee sucks, there suck I;
In a cowslip's bell I lie;
There I couch when owls do cry.
On the bat's back I do fly
After summer merrily.
Merrily, merely shall I live now
Under the blossom that hangs on the bough."
(Shakespeare's, *The Tempest*, Act V, Scene I).

Are we to think that the merit of the above lines rests outside its art? Is a convincing impossibility preferable to an unconvincing possibility (Aristotle, 1984,

Book 25, p. 2339)? However fantastical Shakespeare's language appears, some of the value of it for teaching is in its imaginative splendour. Vividly presented, Ariel's enchanting imagery can act as a kind of regeneration of the world, an elemental evocation of being dreamily alive in the discourse of living. One feels emotionally the temperance of Ariel's joyful mood. Shakespeare's lines evoke a gentle world that may deepen a student's experience.

Naturally, we would be most disturbed by any student who attempted to present in a painting, sculpture, dance, film, or story the admiration of a rape. A morally repugnant attitude displayed in an artwork will cast a shadow on its value, but it does not follow either that a morally 'good' attitude displayed in an artwork will make us think twice about it. Counterfactually, ought we to accept, though, that there can be a correspondence, for example, between the moral sentiment of a play and its art? The work of Charles Dickens, as much as Emily Brontë and many others, seem to express this connection. Furthermore, if we turn to our chapter in this book on Louis Arnaud Read, we will see have it is impossible to separate out in art teaching practice the interpenetration of moral sentiment.

Nonetheless, what Dewey is further intimating is how the ordinariness of life aesthetically experienced may also recommit us to a deepening ethical sense of existence. Our "tangled scenes of life are made more intelligible in aesthetic experience" (Dewey, 1980, p. 290), because artistic perception is the product of a "clarified, coherent, and intensified or 'impassioned' experience" (Dewey, 1980, p. 290). He does not believe, like many have, that aesthetic experience is specious but rather "directly precious" (Dewey, 1980, p. 293) because its mode of sense is proper to experience, truth, and spiritual being. For example, "Courbet often conveys the essence of a liquidity that saturates a landscape; Claude, that of the *genius loci* and of an arcadian scene; Constable, the essence of simple rural scenes of England; Utrillo, that of the buildings in a Paris street. Dramatists and novelists construct characters that extricate the essential from the incidental" (Dewey, 1980, p. 293-4). So "instead of fleeing from experience to a metaphysical realm, the material of experience is so rendered that it becomes the pregnant matter of a new experience" (Dewey, 1980, p. 294). Similar to Aristotle, aesthetic experience is then defined by Dewey as a "mode of knowledge" (Dewey, 1980, p. 290).

Clearly, teaching has a moral duty of care, but what Dewey is also saying is that if we were to take Sophocles' *Antigone*, for example, the effect of this poetic drama confronts us agonisingly with some of the customs and morality of ancient Greek society. We come to imagine Antigone's strife intensely, compassionately, and comprehensively because Sophocles is able to paint a picture of her which is full of human pathos and thought. Underlying the human common qualities which we perceive as real in the drama is to note the spirit of the poem's sanity and pertinence. The movement of the artist's subject matter and the scenes we recognise as being part of our world in *Antigone* are, as Dewey stresses, being held together by our imaginative depth in direct proportion to the work's arrangement and articulation. Sophocles realistically captures the difficulties and suffering of Antigone's life. His description of Antigone is full of the kind of tension and tragic realism that can go on in our lives. Alone, Antigone feels that the state law is terribly unjust. In despair she chooses death, rather than life. We experience the interhuman in the play because the play creates a genuine conversational dialogue. Though fictional the play is commensurate with human experience, and reminiscent of how we might envisage events in the world unfolding when juxtaposed against certain political, ethical and social demands. As we read *Antigone,* we become acting participants in it as if we were being "lifted by our imagination into a union" (Todes, 2001, p. 143) with the play's dilemma. Sophocles never depersonalises, prearranges, undermines, or withdraws the very vital reciprocity, self-realisation, and human existence of Antigone. The characters in the play appear natural and true. This is part of the play's art: a "fiction that signifies great things" (Da Vinci 1989), the causes of which are dependent upon an art education that can invoke "the power of what is most deep-lying" (Dewey, 1980, p.71) in the control of the artistic material. Conflict and awakening may seem at the heart of Sophocles's depiction of Antigone. This means for Dewey an art education nourished by life's understanding of sensitive imaginative creation and perception. We must be careful not to suggest from this that artistic imagination and perception are outside of the true and the false. The Aristotelian argument pertaining to imitation, as we have seen, would exploit the fact that Sophocles' *Antigone* as poetic drama enacts that "which the direct speech of agents gets us as near as language can come to the nature of significant action itself" (Halliwell, 1998, p. 54).

Two further claims are worth making about Sophocles' *Antigone* and about art education in general that reinforce Dewey's examination. Firstly, Aristotle remarks: "though the objects themselves may be painful to see, we delight to view the most realistic representations of them in art" (Aristotle, 1984, Book 4, p. 2318). The second point is that the delight that we can take from art can be "at the same time learning—gathering the meaning of things, e.g. that the man there is so-and-so" (Aristotle, 1984, Book 4, p. 2318). If we were to reduce a tragic play simply to the level of its morality without its aesthetic imagistic qualities, without its moments of pleasure and excitement, for instance, we would not be talking about how Dewey perceives art as relevant for education. Like Aristotle, Dewey believed that the character and the life of people as "they do and suffer" (Aristotle, 1984, Book 1, p. 2316) indicated some of the natural form of art education. In a Deweyan manner a work like Sophocles' *Antigone* embodies the collective and individual experience of a culture that is sometimes the most difficult to observe and feel. The effect of this work connected with the problems it presents helps to break down physical isolation and external contact bringing to pass our own experience, and reorientation. This shows important consequence for Dewey, that art education can have an instrumental value "operating in indirect channels" (Dewey, 1980, p. 139).

Art creation sometimes runs ahead of the true and the false, using imaginative methods and experiences in the world to express the character of the event under scrutiny with determinateness. "Poetry celebrates the diversity of the human soul, but philosophy inculcates the correct principles of the best life" (Rosen, 2005, p. 354). Hence, in "this sense, poetry is like democracy, whereas philosophy is like monarchy" (Rosen, 2005, p. 354). What Dewey realised, succinctly expressed by Ernst Gombrich, but which Plato's epistemology logically found of third-division status was if: "we look out of the window we can see the view in a thousand different ways" (Gombrich, 1977, p. 331). The photograph, dance, poem or story which the student creates from looking out of the window "is charged with meanings that issue from intercourse with a common world" (Dewey, 1980, p. 306). The thousand and more ways to paint the view from an art class window means for Dewey that the student has to properly interrogate and express their genuine thoughts, perceptions, and feelings that are integral to what is being perceived. This life which affects the art-making process in education is not necessarily governed by general principles in the way that moral judgements might be. Our imagination, which comes from out of our lives, may be morally reprehensible but for Dewey its content may open questions of unrest as well as ease which he sees as being a check on society that also serves to attend to the enterprise of what an actualising and positive culture is supposed to be democratically. On this view, art education can have preparatory and instrumental value for moral contemplation.

As revelation externalised, art education teaches us further how to love life by the particular way it handles and transforms children's vision. The relation between art and morality is one firm dimension of this. Yet another equally important orientation for Dewey is how the child creates a stormy sky in their drawings or creates an embroidery motif in a sample of cloth that in each case shows the child's own sovereign attention to their work mingled with the spirit of their lives (Tanner, 2003). Aesthetic sensibility and training is not all-out moral sensibility and training. In Sophocles' *Antigone*, we have discussed how Sophocles organises his language with a style that expresses the story's sensory reality. But this cannot account for the ethical excellence of a lived life that presupposes something much more than "two apples, an onion, a pair of old shoes,...A couple of notes, a couple of musical notes. And suddenly it is as if the Absolute itself were hanging on the wall or in the air, radiating in all its splendour" (Comte-Sponville, 2005, p. 105). The sensory reality of two apples, an onion, a pair of old shoes and a couple of musical notes move towards "its own consummation through a connected series of varied incidents" (Dewey, 1980, p. 43). We tend to see art education as a fulfilment of the child's concrete human interaction with their imagistic capabilities. Its strength lies not in exercising principles whose moral purpose can burden art to the abstract and hence not art at all, but in eliciting imaginative vision through artistic devices that are open to aesthetic qualities in experience "which from it proceeds the liberating and uniting power of art" (Dewey, 1980, p. 349). Dewey does not see art education as having to be allegorical in kind, of which Goya's *The Nude Maja* (1800) is a case in point. So, while he favours an art education accompanied by sensitiveness to moral sentiment, reasoning, and behaviour, he also sees that art as an experience sets out from a human living context that cannot be subsumed by moral unfolding alone. It is essential to art education autonomy, in fact, that a song, dance, "poem and picture present material passed through the alembic of personal experience" (Dewey, 1980, p. 82), which, as he further realises, concerns not overlooking one's own experience and integration of it. A process which he goes on to surmise enables the child to undergo and present to the world new experiences and meanings.

When Dewey claims that "the political and economic arts that may furnish security and competency are no warrants of a rich and abundant human life, save as they are attended by the flourishing of the arts that determine culture" (Dewey, 1980, p. 345), he is surmising that what the arts bring into a democratic social system of education is a richly endowed process of imaginative approbation that touches the emotions, values, and desires of people in ways our political, moral, and economic fundamentals cannot possible supply. "The imaginative endures because, while at first strange with respect to us, it is enduringly familiar with respect to the nature of things" (Dewey, 1980, p. 269). Our own imaginative capacity relates to our perceiving ability, experience as experienced in the social life of beings. Humanity cries out for art because it satisfies and reinforces many common and quite ordinary qualities that have a special place in our lives in aesthetic perceptive ways. The child's expressive acts in art education are fused with the qualities of their human becoming being stirred by the channels of "internal and intrinsic integration" (Dewey, 1980, p. 99), whose efforts are reaching for things and "directing locomotion" (Dewey, 1980, p. 100), bleeding with the common culture which manifests our own experience.

Can we disagree with Dewey when he maintains that our first "intimations of wide and large redirections of desire and purpose are of necessity imaginative" (Dewey, 1980, p. 349)? If, for example, we cannot imaginatively see the problems, pleasures and anxieties of our students, what kind of relationships with them can we have? While human production often requires imagination for technical and commercial usages, art, paradoxically, "is looked upon with distrust" (Dewey, 1980, p. 348), and in a world where "social divisions and barriers exist, practices and ideas that correspond to them fix meter and bounds, so that liberal action is placed under restraint" (Dewey, 1980, p. 348). He argues that if art were "an acknowledged power in human association and not treated as the pleasuring of an idle moment or as a means of ostentatious display, and were morals understood to be identical with every aspect of value that is shared in experience, the 'problem' of the relation of art and morals would not exist" (Dewey, 1980, p. 348). The individual experiences of the student viewed as freely self-moving, immediate, and common in respect to their own location will show their artistic reasoning to be morally imperfect. Yet, is this necessarily a flaw, given what art education as experience can absorb into itself as an expansion of our own being fostering a communities shared intimate life? To think that life can be divided up into only good and bad features, right and wrong, the criminal and the saint, black and white, whiter than white, and "sheep and goats" (Dewey, 1980, p. 348) suggests to Dewey that if moral beliefs are determined in this way, they will inhibit human flourishing and the forgetting of a child with his or her own horizon and perceptual experience of the world.

As claimed, Dewey's thesis relates to the way our environment governs art education. It is characteristic of our environment that "experience is a matter of the interactions of organism with its environment that is human as well as physical, that includes the material of tradition and institutions, as well as local surroundings" (Dewey, 1980, p. 246). Art education projects itself through its environment and is, in turn, affected by it in a common community of life. An environment that is democratically interacting and socially concerned for art stands in response to it and becomes enlightened by it. Our life is dependent on its environment, so that our environment survives in the concrete comprehension and many-faceted world of human experience. The greatest threats and possibilities for art education must, therefore, come from what our environment holds.

Consequently, according to Dewey, an environment which minimises human experience will reinforce intolerances not suited for the expansion of human sympathies. Differences become difficult to tolerate and for the child deprived of difference, becoming different by "what grows by itself" (Irigaray, 2002, p. 112) is part of what Luce Irigaray goes on to say is the real aspect of becoming. Maxine Greene notes that the supporting structures that exist in education "are not used to sustain a sense of agency among those they shelter; instead, they legitimate treatment, remediation, control—anything but difference and release" (Greene, 1995, p.41). Submitting simply to authority will prevent the child from knowing themselves. If we block the process that lets the teacher in to the secrets of the child's life, how can they find ways that will inspire and acknowledge the child's existence? Dewey thought that only a free and equal society could attain the capacity and compulsion to enter the interests of another culture, a process that involves a serious interaction with art, without which he envisages that a community's lifestyle cannot cope with proper democracy, liberalism, and choice. How does art help democracy, liberalism, and choice? He reasons that a society will succeed as an environment imperfectly and govern itself incompetently if it cannot take unto itself a multitude of different perspectives that would make it rich in the arts of living experience. He is insistent that art should express freely the world we encounter in everyday existence as concretised gestures of human fulfilment. A vital part of education comes from what originates from children themselves as cumulative with their continuous unfolding and momentum in the world. Art education blossoms in an educational environment, argues Dewey, when it is infused with ordinary experiences that are natural to it, so that "the attitudes of the self are informed with meaning" (Dewey, 1980, p. 59). Art education must form a symmetry with life because this is the condition for having an experience of art that helps to refine and support democratic, liberal, and changing values.

Now, Dewey criticises art theory and connoisseurship for having developed critiques centering on the power of stardom, categorisation, bourgeois culture, manipulation, and intellectualism, which have put aside daily living, the feeling of poetry, the skin of emotion, the touch of petals, thorns, silks, and bodies. The ultimate test of any aesthetic experience for Dewey is in the actual, embodied meaning, as expressed in the common lives of people. However, he saw that the world of art is divided up between rich taste and poor taste, between high culture and low culture. There is the exhibitionism of art as an economic and culturally intellectual marketing tool. There is the art lover who owes his education to the

Louvre or the Tate Modern. We have the collector of art in search of rare items and the nouveau riche lifestyles displayed in countless newspapers and magazines. Likewise, we have the division of art between the contemplative and the useful arts and the wealth and celebrity status of individuals to determine prices and trends in art. There are the forces of nationalism, sectarianism, and purism that in different ways for him have further weakened the connection that "aesthetic perception is in the concrete" (Dewey, 1980, p. 10). When life is full of dangers and opportunities, when life can be narrow or widened, art feeds human experience making it "possible to carry to new and unprecedented heights that unity of sense and impulse" (Dewey, 1980, p. 22), that of fulfilment, continuity, and enrichment which is needed to avoid a segregating, unpleasureable, unspeaking, and unopening world.

Enriched by a repertoire of power and indifference the art world and the wider community, Dewey comments, both have downgraded aesthetic experiences. Art education has meaning only when: "instruction in the arts of life is something other than conveying information about them. It is a matter of communication and participation in the values of ordinary life by means of the imagination, and works of art are the most intimate and energetic means of aiding individuals to share in the arts of living. Civilisation is uncivil because human beings are divided into non-communicating sects, races, nations, classes and cliques" (Dewey, 1980, p. 336).

The net effect of all this, Dewey thinks, has been a betrayal of the human subject in art as the common normal experience for art education. Under these circumstances, he maintains, art education becomes deprived of its opening. Collapsed are the shared properties of life which may be active in art education as an experience through the whole person. Withered and now marginalised, art education as life positive finds itself in a dry well, bereft of normal aesthetic experiences. Life will then, for Dewey, press forward "anesthetic" living (Dewey, 1980, p. 62). When this happens, he intimates that art education becomes the economy of being, frail and an arbour of self-deprivation that then heightens unconsciously an inactive sense of our own bodies and that of the other. The lowering of poetic experience in art education Dewey interprets as a lowering of education achievement generally. The positive educational pathway that reunites living in relation to the environment for Dewey is when "vivid aesthetic experience" (Shusterman, 1995, p. 35) more effectively connects art education with our social life and human becoming. These vivid aesthetic experiences, he believes, help to safeguard ordinary experiences that add to the harmony, beauty, unity and creativity in our environment.

Aesthetic education starts "with the soil, air, and light out of which things aesthetically admirable arise" (Dewey, 1980, p. 12). The delightful sounds of a student playing the violin, the excitement of seeing a great grey owl, of smelling fragrant mornings when the air is full of scent, the compassion of children playing together, a hummingbird knocking its beak against one's window, the measured way a student leaves visible in their painting a rock's shape through colour, a poem written by a student recording his love for his mother, the sweet touch of a father's kiss on his son's cheek as his son goes to school, jet black pebbles found on a beach, the reading of a fairy tale, the pride taken in ancestral knowledge, or the angelic voices of a school's choir resonating along its corridors. Here we have the tangible significance of celebrating, the "valuable in things of everyday enjoyment" (Dewey, 1980, p. 11) but which may come as an extra rather than as the normal and substantive involvement of art and education in our environment. The Maori statues on Easter Island, Michelangelo's *Creation of Adam*, Rodin's *Kiss*, Picasso's *Guernica,* and Albert Camus' *The Outsider* are just a few of the many thousands of examples that if we had time for in our deliberations would demonstrate how art does not isolate itself from the concrete world of reality and human becoming.

To summarise, Dewey is reminding us that the generative nature of art as experience starts with aesthetic perceptions. Conversely, he claims that a student may well "undergo sensations as mechanical stimuli or as irritated stimulations, without having a sense of the reality that is in them and behind them: in much of our experience our different senses do not unite to tell a common and enlarged story. We see without feeling; we hear, but only a second-hand report, second hand because" (Dewey, 1980, p. 21) it is not visual evidence on the listener's part. Dewey goes on to enlighten us further of our aloofness in life: "we touch, but the contact remains tangential because it does not fuse with qualities of senses that go below the surface. We use the senses to arouse passion but not to fulfil the interest of insight, not because that interest is not potentially present in the exercise of sense but because we yield to conditions of living that force sense to remain an excitation on the surface" (Dewey, 1980, p. 21). Art education intervenes, maintains Dewey, to push through the values of ordinary deep experience.

We are now at the stage where we can indicate the factors which should influence an art syllabus on Dewey's lines:

- The art teacher must produce "a change that will reduce the force of external pressure and will increase that of a sense of freedom and personal interest in the operation of production" (Dewey, 1980, p. 343). A teaching approach where the vision and the production is the student's expressed work. To teach in ways knowing what the aesthetic brings to life and the resistant and tensional forces which can affect it. An art education that learns from its past but develops its own means of expression for its own time.
- The art teacher should create important class contact time for doing experimental work. Experimentation, Dewey argues, "open[s] up new fields of experience and disclose new aspects and qualities in familiar scenes and objects" (Dewey, 1980, p. 144). An art education environment where students are encouraged to handle a variety of materials, movements, sounds, styles, metaphors, images, gestures, and ideas in adventurous and unexpected ways. An environment where student are the source of art, exploring the world around them and interacting with it to discover new means of expression, methods of construction, and the production of new objects in a complete, integrating, and unified manner.
- An art education syllabus must be broad based and capable of nurturing fully, intimately, immediately, and energetically the student's intelligent responses to the world. To create a teaching environment where students can share their lives and which brings students together whatever their culture and interests are.

Encouraging human becoming through art education means fostering and enriching the imagination, emotions, perceptions, and desires of students.

- Any syllabus in art education must be constructed to appreciate the preciousness of ordinary experiences. Experience transforms perception and production in artwork shaping the significance that belongs to it. Educational practice and policy must value and protect experience as experience concretely and extensively.
- To facilitate all operations of production in art education where "imaginative vision addressed to imaginative experience (not to set judgment) of possibilities that contrast with actual conditions. A sense of possibilities that are unrealized and that might be realised are when they are put in contrast with actual conditions, the most penetrating 'criticism' of the latter that can be made. It is by a sense of possibilities opening before us that we become aware of constrictions that hem us in and burdens that oppress" (Dewey, 1980, p. 346).
- The freedom to teach and to teach in different consummatory ways which inwardly and outwardly stimulate the forces of art as experience. In this respect, Dewey would insist that while art teaching must be directed towards the student and their yearnings; it must also be concerned with the outside world and the importance of social feeling. Art education at its core values enormously the student's personality but a personality drive seeking only admiration may force a retreat into itself, resulting in too much self-love.
- In negotiation with students, Dewey's art education syllabus implies a set of tasks, exercises, projects, and processes designed to tackle the existing world the student lives in. Producing artworks whose subject-matter, content, and expressiveness is keeping alive the feeling for a common world through experiences rendered by imagination.
- An art syllabus that attends to the poetic content of experience in life as a significant habit-forming aspect of the student's work (Garrison, 1999, p. 216). Such teaching of art values qualitative judgements, "qualities-in-qualitative-relations" (Dewey, 1980, p. 308) concerned with the individual performance or object the student is creating or has created.

II

Art as an Experience and the Teaching of Art

To assure the world of the authentic experience of art education Dewey insists that "to understand the aesthetic in its ultimate and approved forms, one must begin with it in the raw; in the events and scenes that hold the attentive eye and ear of man, arousing his interest and affording him enjoyment as he looks and listens: the sights that hold the crowd—the fire-engine rushing by; the machine excavating enormous holes in the earth" (Dewey, 1980, p. 5). The teaching of art is driven by the students' involvement in the world, the appearance of things and their meanings. These are the provocations that excite visual images and the reciprocal processes of further hearing, touching, and moving that calls forth an emotion, a surge of action, an intensity of thought, a resumption of effort and an enlargement of perception. Thus, as Philip W. Jackson reveals, Dewey's conception of art includes "the continuity between experiences connected with the arts, on the one hand, and ordinary experience on the other" (Jackson, 1995, p.26). The student's "position expresses the poised readiness of the live creature to meet the impact of surrounding forces, to meet so to endure and to persist, to extend or expand through undergoing" (Dewey, 1980, p. 212) responses apart from its own. The handling of direct experiences is how Dewey envisages the initial teaching of art to involve face-to-face direct contact engagement. It is an art education that must be steeped in community life and immediacy. This does not mean to copy, but rather that the world of art making is opened up to leave room for what can ordinarily be shared as an appropriate direct experience in perception. In direct experience the student is free to perceive "those potencies in things" (Dewey, 1980, p. 185) which evoke an aspect of the object in revelatory ways. Direct experiences are concretely accessible and are crammed with real life incidents, culture and reality important for social life. Dewey seems to be saying that any "extraction of what the subject matter has to say" (Dewey, 1980, p. 92) to us, should emanate from under the circumstances of direct experience in art education.

A few words are needed to explain how Dewey defines experience. There is a difference between an experience proper and the mere sensation of an experience which he describes as inchoate. "Things are experienced but not in such a way that they are composed into an experience" (Dewey, 1980, p. 35). He is trying to show at this stage that the vague sensation of an experience fails to create a meaningful practical perception. "Things happen, but they are neither definitely included nor decisively excluded" (Dewey, 1980, p. 40). A vague sensation is an indistinguishable experience that does not live in our power to determine. It represents "no genuine initiation and conclusion" (Dewey, 1980, p. 40). It is without distinction. He invites us to think of this notion as an uneducated experience because it fails to exercise understanding and obligation.

On the other hand, an educational experience is an "organized" (Dewey, 1980, p. 40) interchange of effective action, self-movement and determination. It interacts with its environment knowingly, deliberately, consenting to it and alert of it. In recognition of Dewey, Harry S. Broudy writes of an experience that it "has a beginning, a development, a climax, and a resolution that rounds it off, thus making it stand out" (Broudy, 1994, p.33–34). The educational point for Dewey is that experience "is the result, the sign, and the reward of that interaction of organism and environment which, when it is carried to the full, is a transformation of interaction into participation and communication" (Dewey, 1980, p. 22). An experience therefore is memorable, connecting, accumulating, complete, and accomplishing. It often has a comprehending qualitative dimension: "a unity that gives it a name, that meal, that storm, that rupture of friendship" (Dewey, 1980, p. 37) or 'remember that dance routine we performed at school yesterday'.

In *Art as Experience* 'undergoing' and 'doing' are key words that are continuously utilised by Dewey to further prove how an educated experience takes effect. The 'undergoing' element refers to receptivity, while the 'doing' element refers to action. Undergoing and doing form a relationship, a synergy in experience whose pattern and structure creates a perception. Perception requires, Dewey argues, the interaction of undergoing and doing because this relationship produces perceptual activity and its consequences. Furthermore, "experience is limited by all the causes which interfere with perception of the relationship between undergoing and doing" (Dewey, 1980, p. 44). Perceptual insight is in proportion to the "scope and content of the relationships measure the significant content of an experience" (Dewey, 1980, p. 44). "A child's experience may be intense, but, because of lack of background from past experience, relations between undergoing and doing are only slightly grasped, and the experience does not have great depth or breadth" (Dewey, 1980, p. 44). Dewey insists that infrequent or excessive undergoing or doing will distort the student's perceptions, when what is always needed is a balance. However, undergoing and doing must form part of the necessary habit activity of art practice in education that governs unity. Perception is the decisive action that is required in art activity. But why is this? "A painter must consciously undergo the effect of his every brush stroke or he will not be aware of what he is doing and where his work is going" (Dewey, 1980, p. 45). The doing and undergoing must be carried out "to the whole that he desires to produce" (Dewey, 1980, p. 45). There is a temptation here, however, to overemphasise the process of conscious undergoing and the finish product the student desires. Nevertheless, the qualitative differences we encounter in experiences that impact on our seeing, hearing, reading, dancing, and making can give rise to further differences in thoughts, ideas, emotions, and performances. Qualitative differences in art education elevate creative vision and lure the child into taking relevant action, the experience of which can modify and result in more sensuous, expressive, and imaginative presentations. All this happens within the framework of undergoing and doing, "as we manipulate, we touch and feel, as we look, we see; as we listen, we hear. The hand moves with etching needle or with brush. The eye attends and reports the consequences of what is done" (Dewey, 1980, p. 49).

Dewey affirms that "an environment that is changed physically and spiritually demands new forms of expression" (Dewey, 1980, p. 303). Where "the very meaning of an important new movement in any art is that it expresses something new in human experience, some new mode of interaction of the live creature with his surroundings and hence the release of powers previously cramped or inert" (Dewey, 1980, p. 303–4). However, this new vision must indispensably protect itself by a "deliberate openness to life itself" (Dewey, 1980, p. 304). From this point of view the student's vision will become contrived or corrupted if it is not seriously open to human challenges. Certainly the student in art education must be allowed to go their own way and "evoke the energy appropriate to its realization" (Dewey, 1980, p. 178) secured by a vision which is cooperative and completed by life. The art critic Mel Gooding on the painter Patrick Heron writes that: "shaping and re-shaping the house and its unique garden, he has been shaped by it; in occupying it, it has come to occupy him; it has become the ground of his creative being, the very centre of his vision and his imaginings" (Gooding, 2002, p. 8). Art education is a sponge as well as a fountain.

Some further enunciations of the common in my above remarks are in order. Dewey makes it plain that the "material out of which a work of art is composed belongs to the common world rather than to a self, and yet there is self-expression in art because the self assimilates that material in a distinctive way to reissue it into the public world in a form that builds a new object" (Dewey, 1980, p. 107). In a number of his quotes already mentioned the common world involves those valuable things found in everyday enjoyment; like fixing a child's bicycle or those moments when the teacher tells us a story that helps to light up the world for us. It is a good custom, argues Iris Murdoch in *The Sovereignty of Good over Other Concepts*, to see the world as it is and to look at these things which give light as discernibly important. Murdoch maintains that these things are precious to others and with oneself. In this way art education exhibits for Dewey less of life's automatic rigid functioning and more of what is overflowing in children's and adults' perceptions that show how art as an experience unites people "in origin and destiny" (Dewey, 1980, p. 271).

Implicit in his conception of direct experience is one's connecting immediate experience. In the normal course of events we thrive upon our immediate experiences, an instance of which is the student's spontaneity in the making of their artwork. Unconstrained, unmediated, and unforced as this human action may be, the poet William Wordsworth is quite specific about it, mentioning in his preface to the *Lyrical Ballads* that immediate experiences in art have a 'distinct purpose" (Wordsworth, 1907, p. 935). When he sums up immediate experience as "the spontaneous overfull of feelings" (Wordsworth, 1907, p. 935), we are taken by this intentional artistic expression but this is a less than transparent statement, since it designates on first view only the subjective.

Wordsworth clears the air for us by explaining how immediate experience can operate in art making in a practical way. He reveals how immediate experience is: (1) a "submission to a necessity" (Wordsworth, 1907, p. 954), (2) a "state of subjection to an external object" (Wordsworth, 1907, p. 954), and (3) a response to "objects as they exist and as re-acted upon by one's own mind" (Wordsworth, 1907, p. 954). Wordsworth adds that immediate experience in art creation requires "a fashioning through imagination" (Wordsworth, 1907, p. 934), and the "impression of sense" (Wordsworth, 1907, p. 955), which are "from repeated and regular feelings" (Wordsworth, 1907, p. 935) that get "modified and directed by other thoughts" (Wordsworth, 1907, p. 935). Immediate experiences are susceptible to the "shifting scenery of the mind" (Wordsworth, 1907, p. 955). It would be an inaccuracy to conceive the 'shifting scenery of the mind' as an arbitrary process because the 'shifting scenery of the mind' is being governed by undergoing, doing, and perception.

An immediate experience comes into its own when as Wordsworth comments: "the more versatile the fancy the more original and striking" the image (Wordsworth, 1907, p. 955). From habit forming, prior experiences, imagination, interrogation, and "patient observation" (Wordsworth, 1907, p. 955), Wordsworth, like Dewey, feels that a student's immediate experiences are developed successively through self-movement. The overall effect is that these "processes of the imagination are carried on either by conferring additional properties upon an object, or [by] abstracting from it some of those which it actually possesses and thus enabling it to re-act upon the mind which hath performed the process, like a new existence" (Wordsworth, 1907, p. 956). Wordsworth is insistent that we have to be enthused, be endowed, and take "delight in the spirit of life" (Wordsworth, 1907, p. 937) in order to avoid "vulgarity and meanness" (Wordsworth, 1907, p. 937). Art education explores immediate experiences in order to see what gives the suspense and what bursts through actions, emotions, and thoughts. In the activity of art as an experience, coalesced are the constant comings and goings of individualised performances and visualisations, "through successive deeds there runs a sense of growing meaning conserved and accumulated towards an end that is felt as the accomplishment of a process" (Dewey, 1980, p. 39) .

Suffice to say that what we should be attending to as teachers are the life moments that occupy children when they are playing in the school's playground. When two children are playing a game of chess at school, when the children are handling spiders in a science class, when there is the school's performance of a Christmas pantomime, and when one of the school's classes visits a nature reserve. Experienced in imaginative ways these events and their impact on the child can drive and renew when rendering such incidents in representative and enacting ways, a love for ordinary life. These experiences define art education by showing art education to be alive to their scenes and meanings. A student in an art class is not only trained to notice these things but is also taught how to create a synergy of life and a synthesis of vitality that achieves a particular integration of receptivity and doing. A student who paints, performs, or writes a poem about their grandmother, friend, toothache, or cups on the table may be handling the ordinary with the particular feelings and thoughts of the child pursuing a common reality of educational practice.

To absorb life through direct immediate contact and to be aroused concomitantly by ordinary experiences which we can all share and value in different ways, are part of that ethos which characterises some of our social human warmth. If we doubt this then we doubt some of the real life of children's growth. In moments when we doubt this and try to suppress these incidents as trivial in the world perhaps, then, we need to remind ourselves of its preciousness. Never withdrawn from view in the Lascaux Caves, for example, is ordinary life. Yet, what we are interested in knowing is why the Lascaux Cave paintings are more than a pathetic truth of the ordinary? The artwork on the walls and ceilings in the Lascaux caves show in some detail not just the anatomical correctness of different animals—their knees, tendons, hoofs,…and tongues—in a realistic fashion, but something further approaching an art which "explodes with a dark, blind power. Even Goya's paintings of bullfights are but a vague echo of this passion" (Herbert, 1985, p. 11). Present in these artistic images are significant human experiences that are the sensitive wrestling of the perceptions they reveal. Images that are not just the finesse of execution in expression but a commitment to a higher aim operating as furtherance and accumulation, rendering an experience unified in a movement of intrinsic fulfilment (Dewey, 1980, p. 146). Would we say that these Lascaux artists have demonstrated, in their image-making constructions, a care for the human as the universal in the particular (Aristotle 1984, Book ? p. 2322)? Reflecting on his time in the Lascaux caves, it dawns on the poet Zbigniew Herbert the inner certitude of a communal perspective which imprints a human face and a concrete world that opens "to the Greek temples and the Gothic cathedrals. I walked towards them feeling the warm touch of the Lascaux painter on my palm" (Herbert, 1985, p. 17).

We have examined how art education responds when it is in contact with the world involving a student that acts and is acted upon. This means that effective art teaching relies on a correspondence between the standards peculiar to art itself and the standards desired by our cultural, institutional and ordinary experiences. Art education proves its worth mobilised by morality and mobilised by the child's own imaginative acts informed by materials, perceptions, and ideas that are reciprocally grasped and gathered in sensitive, tangible, and accountable expressive ways as communal life that is close to us and widespread. The child is trained to form habits, limitations, meanings, and values in distinct purposeful ways. Direct and immediate experiences are at the forefront of Dewey's proposal for teaching art in education. As discussed, different visions in art education relate to the forces operating in its environment as well as to the internal mechanisms, processes, and imaginative experiences that help the student to release and expand his or her own natural abilities to produce artwork which are steeped in the "underlying common elements of the experienced world" (Herbert, 1985, p. 248).

Our ordinary experiences have a natural dynamic for Dewey whose impulse, when dwelled upon and lived, affects the gestures, attitudes, and the reality of the child. In everyday experiences the elements of commonality and continuity of life are found. Social living is a key factor of Dewey's democratic thinking. Art goes deeper than we think, and its human scent is felt strongly in the sweetness of ordinary scenes, when poems, performances, and pictures of daily life consummate the culture of social living, giving it much needed embrace. Art education in this sense reassures us surely of some of the truth of being that constantly needs rescuing. How tender, beautiful, and uniting is our world, and just how aware are we of what summons the qualities of real love in society? If Dewey is right, art education must operate from the child's own aesthetic experiences to unite, break-open, free, and excite our modern sentiment for social living. It is the warmth of our aesthetic lives valued qualitatively in art education, which lovingly brings out the character of our world to benefit social living. Dewey, on the one hand, feels that the child's engagement in ordinary experiences presents ever-fresh challenges for creative artwork, and on the other hand, that these experiences are earnestly important for the well-roundedness of a human being. His theory makes sense because it demonstrates the child's creative involvement in undergoing and doing to generate an integrated, completed, and satisfying everyday experience of its subject matter in art educational practice. By explaining what art as an experience is, Dewey has further answered how art in education can produce a flourishing understanding of the temperament of its society. Not only does he show the development of experience in art education and the value of it, but he also discerns how art education can be instrumental. His claim that art education can make an enormous human contribution to democratic, social, and human understanding still stands out as a test for our education system.

CHAPTER 3

ART AS THE BASIS OF EDUCATION

Herbert Read

"Art leads the child out of itself' (Read, 1944, p.2).

Abstract

Throughout his career Herbert Read worked tirelessly for peace in the world. At
the time when he was working with UNESCO during its infancy he was already
exploring the idea of art-for-peace. A prolific writer, editor, poet, academic, teacher,
curator, activist, art reviewer, historian, and defender of children, Read is one of
education's towering figures. His educational thinking was based on a lifetime of
research in psychology, psychoanalysts, poetry, philosophy, educational theory,
and children's art. In 1943 at the height of his powers, Read shook the educational
establishment with his book Education Through Art. This publication marked a
turning point and is still one of those few historic benchmarks that actually mean
something in the culture of education. In this chapter I will pursue Read's conception
of Education Through Art. I will be arguing that what children embody through
their art, as Read thought, represents part of the filial bond of education. Read's
particular insight into this filial bond is an aspiring account of the virtues of
aesthetic education.

Introduction

The first half of this chapter will debate Read's art as the basis of education and in
the second half of this chapter we will discuss children's art experience as he saw it
in teaching. Read was attempting to proclaim in a way many others have not
attempted to proclaim, why art should be considered as the basis of education. I
believe the time is right to revisit and debate Read's notion that art should be the
basis of education.

Call me a dinosaur, but I sometimes wonder selfishly whether anyone recently
has taken the trouble to read Read's *Education Through Art*. Undoubtedly, this
work is not contemporary, and yes, from where we are now educationally, there are
outstanding problems with it. Malcolm Ross describes *Education Through Art* "as
a pot-pourri of theoretical speculations, and propaganda, a bewildering muddle of
pseudo-science, sympathetic magic, and mystical transcendentalism" (Ross, 1998,
p. 209). Finding myself agreeing with Ross's assessment here, I nevertheless also
want to escape from it. So much so that I believe it is still possible to reach other
conclusions about this book, namely that it advocates a more earthly sense of

49

measure and judgement: a yearning towards children and society. Elliot Eisner's analysis of Read's vision is quite different from Ross's: "I concur that the aim of [all] education ought to be conceived of as the preparation of artists" (Eisner, 2006, p. 208), and by that Eisner means children who have learnt to "develop the ideas, the sensibilities, the skills, and the imagination, regardless of the domain in which an individual works" (Eisner, 2006, p. 208).

Read cuts an unusual figure, one from the mould of Karl Marx, William Godwin, Friedrich Nietzsche, George Orwell, Aneurin Bevan, Tony Crossland, William Wordsworth, Samuel Coleridge, Charlotte Brontë, Charles Dickens, and Ralph Waldo Emerson all poured into one cast. Read's last article *My Anarchism,* a mainstay of his thinking, was published in 1968, the year he died at the age of seventy-five. Although there are numerous influences on Read in *Education Through Art* ranging from Sigmund Freud, Carl Jung, Jean-Jacques Rousseau, and Friedrich Schiller, concomitantly we must not forget how Read branches out to see children's art: "I am in the presence of a poetic truth, a truth which only the child could have expressed" (Read, 1970a, p.212).

Education Through Art was an attempt to define why art should be the basis of education and in a practical way he attempts to work out a syllabus "directly appreciable to our present needs and conditions" (Read, 1970a, p.1). It is not my intention in this chapter to reconstruct his solution because *Education Through Art* was first published in 1943 when the world was preoccupied with World War II. The kind of education materials and skills he was advocating in the years immediately following World War II, one would agree, are hardly the agenda for education today. The circumstances, events, and challenges when he was part of the time writing *Education Through Art* are to some extent in marked contrast to the circumstances, events and challenges now operating in education. Jean-Francois Lyotard's 1979 book The *Postmodern Condition: A Report on Knowledge,* for example, describes a very different educational world from Read's (Lyotard, 1984). Lyotard examines how our education system has become a global business whose expertise is economically driven for industrial production, external knowledge, technology, and methodologically operated now for performative predictability.

We should note in passing three things about *Education Through Art.* Firstly, that it predated the UK Butler's Education Act of 1944 and the 1948 Welfare State (NHS) Act, secondly that *Education Through Art* was written at a time when war was still raging in Europe, Africa, and Asia. This did not escape Read: "Against such a vacillating background I have written this book" (Read, 1970a, p. 302).

He was an advocate of social change, a campaigner, and a critic widely regarded in Europe and North America (Goodway, 1998). *Education Through Art* was his attempt to address some of the concerns of education for its time. It may have seemed a blessing that in *Education Through Art,* there is none of the "art activities designed to promote the war effort" (Efland, 1990, p. 231). I suspect that to be handed a copy of *Education Through Art* after the war was the kind of tonic that people openly and secretly desired coming out of a time where there was little "education for freedom" (Read, 1944, p. 31). For Read was breaking new ground with his psychological insights between "deeply felt convictions on the relation between creative expression in art and the prospect of a healthy society" (Read, 1944, p. 231). *Education Through Art* introduced a whole new approach towards art education that was attempting to strike a blow against disillusionment, emotional starvation, inhumanness, aggression, and the invisibility of being in the world.

Education Through Art was reactive, set against divisive values of class and of teaching methods out of step with modern social ideas, a world in desperate need of equality, democracy, liberalism, freedom and opportunity. In *Education Through Art,* Read was trying to answer these needs and to show how art education embodied the impulse of these callings for a new era in social and emotional life. As a significant figure in modernism and progressive educational thinking (Goodway, 1998, and Read and Thistlewood, 1994), he had the courage to speak differently and innovatively. Eisner elucidates how Read and Viktor Lowenfield "believed the arts to be a process that emancipated the spirit and provided an outlet for the creative impulse" (Eisner, 2002, p. 32) important for human development and personal empowerment. This chapter will have to answer whether *Education Through Art,* as David Goodway surmises, is as unrealistic a thesis as some claim it to be (Goodway, 1998a, p. 191).

It was Read's belief that if we had a race to swing open the doors on education in order to inhale its temperament, the first thing we should see is an education absorbed by art because art, he felt, was part of the young child's common identity and would thus help set them on a journey for life. Art education was hitherto to be a vital part of the child's learning experience. He wanted to instigate an educational change where "art should be the basis of education" (Read, 1970a, p. 1). As edifying as this might sound, what makes him think this is true? What evidence does he produce and what is his argument for it? We must find answers to these questions.

My approach is going to try to piece together enough of his thoughts in *Education Through Art,* with further pieces from his other educational writings, to indicate why Read held art to be the basis of education. He proposed that art education should have a leading presence in the school's curriculum. The difficulty we have is that our prejudices about art education and our view of the modern world may stop us from extrapolating why art can be an effective learning experience in the "psychic life of the child" (Adler, 1970, p.23) as the basis of education.

I

Art as the Basis of Education

"It is possible for pupils to go to school for years and learn nothing amounting to an introduction to taking their places in adult society. Hence, the work in personal and group learning is not a dispensable luxury" (Perry, 1992, p.2).

Before we begin, here is an outline that expresses the key components of an art education that Read designates as forming the basis of education:
– Art is a natural activity of every child and relates to the totality of their being and world.

- Art education enhances the child's personality development by helping to complete their social and individual integration and unification of being in the world. In this sense, Read sees art education as an essential part of human becoming.
- "The world influences the child as nature and as society" (Read, 1970a, p. 288). The point Read is asserting is that our nature is a continuance of those factors that are in the world. The world has power over the person we are and arguably, to some extent, therefore, our happiness (Gay, 1995, p.736). The world as nature for Read means that children become education by relationships, and events in the world: "air, light, the life of plants and animals" (Read, 1970a, p.288).
- The teacher's role must be dialogical and be a relationship of love. They are the mediator between the children and their environment (Read, 1970a, p. 294).
- Art education restores the importance of voluntary, instinctive, imaginative, imagistic, feeling, inventive, original, and spontaneous activity.

- In art education the child partakes in experiential, moral, intellectual, cognitive, emotional, and social learning.
- Art education models itself on delivering a multisensory teaching practice.
- Art education gives pleasure, insight, and it inculcates aesthetic relationships and skills.
- It is a practice which grips and reflects some of life's most harmonic, vibrant, transforming, unifying, and rhythmic experiences.
- Art is intrinsic to school life because it is part of the child's real being; their natural, irreducible and projecting desire to experience such communion, enlightenment and production. Read suggests that we can harm the child's educational development if art is not a significant influence on the school's syllabi.

In light of the above outline it seems unsustainable that art education is still not central to education. What are the reasons for this and do they really add up in meaningful ways? With just an hour a week to teach art in primary schools, we would be hard pressed to maintain that we have art as an educative power. The resulting effect of art on the schools programme and children's learning is often negligible. When so little of music, dance, drama, poetry, stories, painting, and craft time is allocated in the general, basic scheme of education, are we to think that art is an unimportant instrument of culture, social being, psychological growth, integration, and the preservation of life? Was Leslie Perry correct in stating that "recent opinionated policy statements point towards a priority interest in the learning of curricular knowledge" (Perry, 1992, p.2)? Are these, as Perry goes on to say, the only critical skills which are necessary for adulthood?

Read notes that education must be "a collecting of means for a specific end, and most of the complaints about our educational system are directed against the adequacy of such means, or the failure to specify clearly enough the ends" (Read, 1944, p.4). These means and ends, Read determines, have not explained how best to inculcate the teaching of moral virtues as a priority in children's education. Art is not "an extra" (Read, 1944, p.7), Read declares and points out that the adequacy of any means and ends in education have to fundamentally include art education if "initiation into this way of life" that is educational, is to be achieved. Can education ever be complete without art? Not for Read. Art education assists the need for social cooperation because, as Read exhumes it "gives rise to a discipline infinitely nearer to that inner accord of harmony" (Read, 1944, p.25), and the collective good. He is endeavouring to show, amongst other things, how art education does not separate the child from their being in the world. "There is a certain way of life which we hold to be good, and the creative activity which we call art is essential" (Read, 1944, p.7) to this way of life. Education for Read is "an initiation into this way of life, and we believe that in no way is this initiation so successfully achieved as through the practice of art" (Read, 1944, p.7). Education will fail if it does not see, as he states, that the "normal creative activity is one of the essentials of a full and balanced development of the personality" (Read, 1944, p.7) which is needed in the teaching of moral virtues. Creative activity for him is crucial to human becoming and intelligibility because at an early age the child's body and mental processes desire the metabolism of art natural to their temperament and life. Thus if we really want an integrated, sensible, clever, and caring child art education is of paramount importance in the manifestation of such a scheme.

A syllabus with a narrow pedagogy produces, argues Schiller, a primitive form of morality that destroys feeling and sensibility and drains us of wisdom (Schiller, 1982, letter 6). Schiller believed that the value of art in education is in the manifold ways it is concordant with the child's active life. Read agrees with Schiller that art teaches the power of free thought and being in the world that is the measure of each individual as they engage their surroundings. The variance of art reciprocally relates to the poetic drive of the child within a social contract of free resolve (Schiller, 1982, letter 3). If knowledge dissociates itself "from the free movement of the poetic faculty" (Schiller, 1982, p.43) that all children possess, how are we, Schiller claims, to safeguard ourselves from error? Schiller believed that art restores humanity by submitting to the different unfolding life of human beings and Read argued correspondingly that if "our bodies can no longer express themselves naturally" (Read, 1970, p. 99), we will have difficulty divulging ourselves and supporting the concept of citizenship (Read, 2002). Like Schiller (Schiller, 1982, letter 4), Read saw art education as a necessary element of our earthly sense of existence which reciprocally opens up the spirit of each individual within themselves to extend, renew, and complete actions that awaken the experience of life important for social cohesion.

To understand more specifically why Read held art to be the basis of education is to notice how the student's early learning manifests the "spontaneous and innately creative imagination of childhood, both as a form of learning and as a function of the organizing powers of the perceiving nervous system" (Cobb, 1993, p.15). For Edith Cobb, art education is an indispensable part of the child's bioaesthetic cultural development. Art education is essential for world building and a fulfilling ground of children's existence that invites, as Cobb believes, greater creativity and meaning through temporal and spatial dimensions. Art is the child's desire to add form and novelty in a search for linguistic, perceptual, bodily and metaphorical significance. It is part of their "unique patterns of sensory learning and the passionate form-creating striving of each and every child" (Cobb, 1993, p.16). She goes on to say that such deep-seated experience helps the child to exploit in open fashion, images of themselves and their environment important for human personality development and education. Cobb remarks that every child creates in order to know and to be. Children's creative drives enable them to construct ways to understand the other and search for more interactive and dynamic strategies to freely speak and create. In art education the child learns effectively to express their own outlooks and explore the world with their sense of wonder which is unlike, as Cobb indicates, the rigidity of adult perceptions.

Cobb describes children's art education as "compassionate intelligence" (Cobb, 1993, p.25). However, in case we get too carried away with thinking that compassionate intelligence is no more than a therapeutic undertaking that sustains little fruitful work. Read succeeds in showing how art education for the child is also "a dynamic and unifying activity, with great potential for the education of our children. The process of drawing, painting, or constructing is a complex one to make a new and meaningful whole. In the process of selecting, interpreting, and reforming these elements, he has given us more than a picture or a sculpture; he has given us a part of himself: how he thinks, how he feels and how he sees" (Lowenfeld and Brittain, 1982, p.3). Howard Gardner makes the point in one of his studies about how Einstein returned "to the conceptual world of childhood: the search for basic understanding unhampered by conventional delineations of a question. Indeed, the very puzzles that he first pursued as a youth—the behaviour of the point of the compass, the 'thought experiment' of riding on a beam of light—later fuelled his most innovative scientific work" (Gardner, 1993, p.10).

Read's exposition is that education strives for a harmonious and integrated individual in society so that each individual can "render mutual aid" (Read, 1944, p.18) to others. What Read is claiming is that in order to render mutual aid the child must possess positive perceptions of life that are the construal of their happiness and love. An angry, cynical, and alienated person will have difficulty rendering mutual aid. A loving person will not. To give mutual aid, education must be founded on a system that can integrate a person into society. The child, for Read, is someone who "affirms uniqueness, and [does] not want to 'die away, and fade into the light of common day'" (Read, 1944, p.18). He reasons that "the first change on the educator, therefore, is to bring the uniqueness of the individual into focus, to the end that a more vital interplay of forces takes play within each organic grouping of individuals—within the family, within the school, within society itself" (Read, 1944, p.18). Indubitable, this is a tall order. Though one breaking point in this tripartite interconnection that affects the success which governs any such harmonisation and integration process in schools is if we take for granted or suppress the child's unique perceptions, visions, thoughts, and ideas. The aim is not to curb the child's uniqueness and gravitas but to integrate the child into society. Not to stamp all over them, force a technique of the real upon them but to make them feel part of society by respecting the living human person they are that thus induces a care for the child's own becoming (Irigaray, 2002) to arrive at feelings, and thoughts, which can render mutual aid. For Read, the "possibilities are first evenly weighed between hatred, leading to crime, unhappiness and social antagonism and love, which ensures mutual aid, individual happiness and social peace" (Read, 1944, p.18).

What can art education do to assist the process of integration into society in harmonious ways without stifling the uniqueness of the individual? To begin with, art education can provide a satisfying space for the child to examine the world and to immediately note what their deepest feelings and intuitions (Read, 1973, p.2) are. Art education being a process, as suggested, that extends the child's under-standing of themselves and their environment in determinate and reliable ways that spring from the scenes, performances and pictures they describe. Art practice being unbounded, the teacher of art, construes Read (Read, 1973, p.6), exchanges, collaborates and arouses the child's curiosity for free choice and clarification. Integration and uniqueness can thus be harmoniously brought together because "art is a personal and satisfying activity at any age, for although the arts are responsible for a greater awareness of the external world, it is also the arts that give vent to the emotions, the joys and fears of life" (Lowenfeld and Brittain, 1982, p.3). The cultivation of socially-minded attitudes and freedom of expression (Read, 1970a, p. 7) with the external world, which was an issue for Dewey too, becomes, for Read, the pattern of art teaching that transforms education, the "reconciliation of individual uniqueness with social unity" (Read, 1970a, p.5).

The relevance of art education is synonymous with the fact that the child's art "is its true passport to freedom, to the full fruition of all its gifts and talents, to its true and stable happiness in adult life. Art leads the child out of itself. It may begin as a lonely individual activity, as the self-absorbed scribbling of a baby on a piece of paper. But the child scribbles in order to communicate its inner world to a sympathetic spectator, to the parent from whom it expects a sympathetic response" (Read, 1944, p. 132). A sympathetic response aids security, confidence, effort, understanding, and courage. More broadly, "a good part of the struggles of mankind centre round the single task of finding an expedient accommodation—one, that is, which will bring happiness—between this claim of the individual and the cultural claims of the group" (Gay, 1995, p. 741). This is why Rollo May says: "[w]e can, in a splurge of individualism, live by our own integrity; or we can, in a splurge of solidarity, identify ourselves with a group or party that takes our decisions for us and decides by its own rules. Either way leads us into error if it neglects the other" (Rollo, 1972, p.254).

Read calls for an art education which can help bridge the gap in harmonious ways between the individual and society. Part of the symmetry which will affect this harmony occurs when art education takes the child seriously and gives them the room to explore and experience relationships with the world and themselves "as each one in relation to the other" (Irigaray, 2002, p.79). Read, similarly to Nietzsche, held that the student's authentic expression in art is the basis of education as it values the faithfulness of a self, the positive reactions of a human being to their environment. Nietzsche's solution to the problem of education was to give men back the courage of their natural drives (Nietzsche, 1968, No.124, p.76). Ultimately, for Nietzsche, "a living thing wants above all to *discharge* its force" (Nietzsche, 1968, No.650, p.344). Can we have an education which does not spring from the notion that the world seen, felt, and interpreted is part of a human movement effectively embedding the child in everyday life?

Drawing further from Aristotle and Plato, Read proposes that education at primary school level should cultivate what is customary to habituate as an excellence. Read sees the cultivation of an already existing excellence to be the child's capacity for aesthetic experience. He then announces that children's active bodies are essential for experience which opens the way to grow in stature. Accordingly, if children are to "get the right nurture and attention" (Aristotle, 1984, Vol. 2, Book 10, p. 1864) to make progress in their artwork, the teacher must keep alive their vigour by reinforcing the sensuality of their own existence, being able to discuss work-related problems with them, and being able to introduce to the children new forms of art. The happy child learns more because their satisfaction rejuvenates desire (Valery, 1989, p. 27). Dismissing the child's comprehension of an object, event, or perform-ance out of hand in favour of a view where everyone is subjected to the same valuation, Nietzsche (1968, No.275, p.157) insists, is what can lead to separation and isolation of the child. "'Beautiful and ugly', 'true and false', 'good and evil'—these distinctions and antagonisms betray certain conditions of existence and enhancement" (Nietzsche, 1968, No. 298, p.168). Read is aware of these issues but believes that the child's natural inclinations for art and their subsequent teaching of it, show the child to be far more willing, accepting, expecting, and able to explore the world infused by their own overwhelming plasticity and flexibility of responses. Children's free expressive work presents knowledge of their environment and how they are looking at the world (Lowenfeld and Brittain, 1982, p. 9).

It is certainly true that Read's thinking would have protested against an education driven by far too much competition, league tables, assessment, and manipulation in schools which can turn out to be disruptive, draining, insensitive, stigmatizing, and elitist (Read, 1966, p.2). Isolation harms the condition for cooperation, collaboration, balanced human behaviour and "estranges the child from his educator" (Adler, 1970, p.15). It is surely a fact that powerlessness has a negative effect on the student's image of themselves their desires, showing, overcoming, speaking, and diversity of life which are neither good for art education nor the school. "We hear children say, 'I can't draw', which prompts Lowenfeld and Brittain to further remark: "we can be sure that some kind of interference has occurred in their lives" (Lowenfeld and Brittain, 1982, p. 8) for the child to believe this. Education through art aims to release what is physically and mechanistically imposed upon the child to teaching which cultivates what the child freely imposes upon themselves.

Martin Heidegger indicates how art making is strengthened by a "letting be" (Heidegger, 2000, p. 140), unconcealment, a self-showing, and emerging from what is hidden. Art expression "must be allowed to remain in its self-containment. It must be accepted in its own steadfastness" (Heidegger, 2000, p. 152). Although Read was unaware of Heidegger's work, he certainly would have agreed with: "[w]hat seems easier than to let a thing be just the being that it is? Or does this turn out to be the most difficult of tasks, particularly if such an intention—to let a being be as it is—represents the opposite of the indifference that simply turns its back upon the being itself in favor of an unexamined concept of Being?" (Heidegger, 2000, p. 157).

Heidegger sees the notion of 'letting be' as a determining factor in the education of the child and reciprocally in their artwork. The child's manner through purposeful self-expression opens the process that confronts vision and the unthinkable idea that may arise from it. Heidegger, remarks "correctness in representation—stands and falls with truth as unconcealment of being" (Heidegger, 2000, p. 177). One further factor of 'letting be' is being in unconcealment is that children can never be of our making "even merely our representations, as it might all too easily seem" (Heidegger, 2000, p. 178). That in 'letting be' constraints are removed, the child is in flight, responding and guiding their art making and when they are in flight, responding and flowing, they disturb what Read calls the "orderly surface of the conventional" (Read, 1970, p.111). In art education Read observes that the child can "give the world all the immediacy and vitality of his intuitions, his perceptions of the instinctual processes of his mind" (Read, 1970, p.111).

What concerned Nietzsche and Freud was how easily society could commonly turn to "false standards of measurement" (Gay, 1995, p.722) in the "true value of life" (Gay, 1995, p.722). Akin to Schiller before him, Read objected to any system of education that operated unknowingly towards the "telling effects" (Read, 1970, p.99) of an aesthetic education, what presents a natural and vivid characterisation of life. A humanistic conception of education would realise that art education does not function to blunt the voice of the child: "art is rather an expression of our deepest instincts and emotions; it is a serious activity whose end is not so much to divert as to vitalize" (Read, 2002, p. 171). Read realised that education could not just be "the handing down from generation to generation of a cultural pattern, expressed in a form that is hierarchic or aristocratic" (Read, 2002, p. 134–5). Because then the only option for students when a culture of this kind is inserted into schools, was for them to pass under the table their own art as they saw it.

In more ways than one, Read follows Rousseau's advice that we should work with the child's growth, habits, and drives, arousing and vivifying, the sensibility of their artistic production. He also agreed with Rousseau that the teacher of art should train the child to feel every element of their nature that makes them sensible of their experiences and existence. In which case, education, Rousseau discerns, "consist[s] less in precepts than in practice" (Rousseau, 2003, p.9) and there is no doubt that Read took this to be true. In *Education Through Art,* Read turns to a number of noteworthy educators of art practice. According to Kenneth Clark, the art teacher Marion Richardson thought that "the skill of art is born of delight—to draw something you do not love is to lose half your skill" (Clark, 1948, p.9). Read (1970a, p.234) was an admirer of Richardson's teaching of art and clearly had some sympathy with Richardson when she wrote: "The happiest thing is when the means, the manner of expression, are born with the idea; but a child must be aware of the rich possibilities of the means. Let us teach him to discover all he can about materials, and make the very handling of them an interest and a delight" (Richardson, 1948). Richardson reiterates Read's thinking more aptly in the following way: "what I hoped for, and I know in part achieved, was to give the children complete confidence in their inner vision their whole habit of looking" (Richardson, 1948, p.15).

H. Caldwell Cook, an English teacher who also influenced Read's thinking, surmised that play "as I mean it, goes far deeper than study; it passes beyond reasoning, and lighting up the chambers of the imagination, quickens the body of thought, and proves all things in action. The study of books, however thorough, may yet remain but superficial, in the sense that there may be no feeling of reality behind it. 'No impression without expression' is a hoary maxim, but even to-day learning is often *knowing* without much care for *feeling*, and mostly none at all for *doing*. Learning may remain detached, as a garment, unidentified with self. But by Play I mean the *doing* anything one *knows* with one's heart in it. The final appreciation in life and in study is to put oneself into the thing studied and to live there *active*" (Cook, 1919, p.16–17). But something else is to be noted here besides play, and that is that learning involves feeling, doing, and the renewing of oneself engulfed in actions and thoughts that have inner force.

Let us recall that art as the basis of education cannot be created in schools based around nominal spells of art submerged in a mass of other 'greater' demands, the effect of which has not the means to deliver art as the basis of education. If schools are to be real social spaces for learning, then changes to their institutional architecture and their syllabi will have to occur. Social learning involves free thinking, acting, and learning from others. Art spaces must be art spaces proper even at the primary level of teaching, not superficial or difficult spaces because art is always interplaying with and sensitive to its space, sound, light, colour, texture, and warmth; it muses over the poetics of space (Bachelard, 1994). Young children are excitable and insatiable human beings and the art room or studio should reflect in a multiplicity of ways the pleasures of creating from a tradition, *sui generis,* and from the necessity of motion that music, dance, crafts, poetry and drama, for example, can offer. Lowenfeld and Britten argue that in art education we "must be able to use our senses freely and creatively and develop positive attitudes towards ourselves and our neighbors for this learning to become effective" (Lowenfeld and Brittain, 1982, p.16).

Art education for Read could never sanction a world of ready-made imposed shapes; the child as the fugitive of its own body. Wilhelm Viola surmises: "when we regard the child simply as a future adult, denying him his own personality, and right to exercise a logic of his own (which from the point of view of the child is truer than ours, and therefore from the very nature of things different from that of the adult), then it is impossible to speak of child art" (Viola, 1936, p.9–10).

II

Children's Art

To repeat, *Education Through Art* was an attempt by Read to demonstrate art teaching as the basis of education and in the previous pages we have outlined some of his reasons for it. We will now turn to explore the kind of practice in children's art that Read supported.

In art education children are capable of registering all manner of things, and detaching from these things their 'true' shape so that their way of looking, moving, playing, and experiencing reflects other meanings and feelings: creative fictions for the 'true' shape of things that supports the idea of art as the basis of education. For example, Viola describes how "a child was in a circus, and afterwards painted an elephant, and painted it purple. Grey did not seem to him the right colour for so exotic an animal" (Viola, 1936, p.32). In this instance, it dawns upon the child that the elephant has a tumultuous spirit, a majestic presence. To symbolise this elephant, purple is chosen to concentrate our thoughts on its magnificence, a gesture that provokes a different representation and with it new meaning and expression, causing us to think again and restore what otherwise may have been blotted out from vision and thought. Unhesitatingly, Read equates this aesthetic act as the child's corresponding "affectionate exhortations" (Read, 1970, p. 217) for this animal which give way to appearances that generate the representation. The representational process that involves working out its image will further alter the child's aesthetic reasoning and feelings. Equally, "a picture of a bird, for example, is not necessarily intended to show how a bird looks, but may express the sensation of flight" (Stern, 1973, p.53). It needs stressing that the child's 'affectionate exhortations' are immensely important in what children do in their art making because it is part of the quality of their experience that discriminates in ways that can further aid their creativity and expression. Furthermore, the child who went to the circus and afterwards painted their elephant purple appears to have done so out of choice, something he or she wanted to do that fulfilled a need that was much more than an emotional release (Arnheim, 1973).

In a quote from Martin Buber in Read's *Education Through Art*: "the child who, lying with half-closed eyes, waits anxiously for his mother to speak to him—his longing springs from something other than the desire for the enjoyment or domination of a human being, and it is also something other than a desire to do something on his own; in face of the lonely night, which spreads beyond the window and threatens to break in, it is the desire to experience communion" (Read, 1970a, p.286). The enjoyment that the child feels here, as Read suggests, is aiming not at superiority but the kind of enjoyment that only human relationships and union with beings can evoke. When a child paints his or her mother and father, they often do so wanting to bring their emotional feelings of their parents into it, as though the painting is meaningless without taking stock of what they are emotionally experiencing. Their desire to reveal what they have in common with their families is charged by feelings which influence their sensory perceptions, elevated style, and pictorial composition. What their artwork means to them from thoughts and perceptions about their 'object' affects correspondingly the making of the artwork. The human being in them is strong, and drama, poetry, stories, and music, for example, advocate not the discouragement of emotions in art but how to enjoy and express them in life enhancing ways.

Like Read, I am convinced that children through art education convey a presence of themselves whose output can appear astonishing but whose talents can be largely overlooked. Read implies that children are quite capable of displaying the zenithal nature of their significant life as their bodies express authentically the force of human actions, voice, and integrity. Children's artwork expresses their deep affectivity as a harmony that is uninhibited, imaginative, and striving. They greet the world with their eyes open, and in so doing, are reluctant to extinguish any of the flame that is the foretaste of their powers as "a process, an operation, a way of engaging with the world" (Ross and Mitchell, 1993, vol. 33, no.2, p. 102)

Art excites the child's body whose distinctive intentional directedness Read registers, as part of the touchstone, unity and base, the circle around them. Through art the child learns to develop their confirmatory thinking that relates to the perception that certain things are inwardly, and outwardly right or wrong in their visual precept, and impulse. Their bodies with effort reach for "what is over the perceptual horizon" (Todes, 2001, p.xix). Read judged art education to be an invitation for children to notice life's material truth. Cobb, like Rudolf Arnheim, surmises that it is within the child's use of "blocks, paints, or any amorphous or semi-structured material (e.g. sand, twigs, and stones), that we can observe the earliest form of an increasing ability to produce ever more complex and structured gestalten" (Cobb, 1993, p.30). The character of art education acknowledges the child's human instincts, its physical actuality, and its inherent temperament that it receives in part from the world and in cooperation with it, all its beauty, happiness, cruelty, and suffering. It was art drawing attention to its human experiences that Read maintains was everything education through art needed to be. In art, the child's own experience, and understanding of themselves is being artistically transformed, the result of their exact expressions of the world. Children's artwork is expressive and thoughtful rather than untidy or chaotic; the heavy traffic of experience, emotion, and imagery.

From another viewpoint, Read also explicates how a sense of purpose can get over the impasse between duty and desire: "the child, before it can manage a pencil or a brush, can with immense pleasure dab its fingers into paint, and transfer the colours, with some sense of purpose, to a clean sheet of paper. Where there is a sense of purpose, there are already the rudiments of a sense of discipline, already the co-operation of muscular reflexes"(Read, 1966, p.115) He indicates that the notion of discipline in art is affected by the child's absorption in their artwork that beckons, relinquishes, and holds onto experiences that overcome great obstacles. He attributes to the educational policy maker A. L. Stone the fact that expression "in the arts gives not only a natural approach to academic subjects, but also a more confident basis for tackling the difficulties of social relationships" (Read, 1966, p.116).

Children produce more than art that hangs on walls, that stands in spaces, that is read out aloud during assembly, or is part of a performance or concert piece; for children are, Read perceives, the very manifestation of art as the basis of education. When children read a story to themselves and appear to be engaged in it, they may be learning about human relationships and human survival even when the story is about *Peter Rabbit*. They are everything that 'correct proportion' is not: the illusion of a perfect statistical model, made up of parts of average size, and shape that can be put together at will. The child's aesthetic experience assumes the form of the child that signifies their conversations with people and things, with words, actions, bodily movement, materials, language, and music. Unconsciously and involuntarily, the child approves of many things that reflect their life. Aesthetic experience is an autotelic activity for the child; one that promotes their immersion, and impressions of the world. Unknowingly, the child may risk everything in an unrestrained aesthetic experience that more vehemently tastes the world, the free play of its psychic forces about to achieve something in the world, to generate itself through the world, and to feel the passion of the world. The child in art experiences stands up and stretches itself, mirrors its being, discovers, searches, clutters, finds, touches, imagines, and thinks. In a drama workshop the child is constantly reasoning, performing, and determining through a plethora of testing experiments and demands.

This aesthetic life of the child is raw, nervous, asserting, and social, is full of formidable insight that art education can exploit. Their frankness, unguardedness, impatience, and quick silvery actions are part of their real relationship to things, a response to sounds, and a reflection of their harmony with existence. We are sensual and difficult beings, and the child understands this well for in their artwork, and in their bodies they give vent to these relations. Within themselves the aesthetic flows with ease. Children, through art experience, bring out into the open a less restricted sense of what gives in their being, exhibiting qualities of life whose configurations express what they are caught up in as sensitive and memorable to themselves. The child's immersion in life and their particular summation of it can escape what sometimes we cannot see as adults in our conservative lives, and thus fail to appreciate the child's artistic impact on the world. How a child constructs the look of the real in their artwork involves the full expressiveness of their psychological capacities, constructed thinking, perceptions, and skills.

The child's aesthetic learning is part of what caresses their life, spurs it on, flirts, scrutinises, and explores, the flourishing tremor of their imagination, and seduction in a present that can create in a moment of intimacy something never seen before. The result of a craving perhaps, or an instinctive urge that naturally wonders about what would happen if I do this...? While often unable to contain themselves, children discern through art that paper, sound, expression, textiles, colour, rhythm, voice, pattern, and language can astonishingly prise open a vision, an end, a problem, and an objection. A line can provoke a memorable world that lifts an elevated mood, a perception, and an unfolding experience. Each rhyme made and each tune played signals an adventure, a light and a discovery of new potential and meaning.

In the occult operations of their drawings the child inscribes the marks of their finitude, solidarity, momentum, and with their touch an attic door may open to invite us into its world, a three-storey house becomes a four-storey house and in another drawing a jet black cat hovers over the head of a long-nosed spiky-haired witch (Read, 1970a, Reproduction no.33, G11) in a beautiful decorative dress to reminds us of the dwelling and imagination of the child. These kinds of drawings have advantages over predetermined constructions, and the information that children leave behind in such work is a testimony of their receiving, giving, and recovering more of their own being in the world in contact with their own making, and view of the world. Children's drawings represent inseparably the living life of their surroundings.

Franz Cizek is one of education's major pioneering art teachers. Read, similarly to Cizek, argued against an education where children are seen as only "pupil-material" (Read, 1970a, p. 212) to be worked upon. Cizek's method is an effective example of art teaching, and is a worthy concept to explore but, to be sure, it is a teaching method not suitable for all forms of art activity. Read was familiar with the example that I am now about to analyse and understood its importance by maintaining an awareness of it in his writings. S.B. Malvern writes of Cizek: "What he rejected was the conventional and academic notion of the teacher as the possessor of some wisdom to be transmitted to the child whose mind was, as it were, a *'tabula rasa'* awaiting the inspiration of prior and predetermined knowledge. In particular, his teaching methods emphasised working from imagination and memory. By using verbal descriptions or stories, Cizek promoted the child's imagination and resourced the child's internal image" (Malvern, 1995, p. 267). In this example, Malvern is referring to Cizek's teaching in Vienna at around 1918-1922. His teaching approach involved creating an environment where children were expected to think for themselves. No rigid schematisations were taught in his art classes. Instead, Cizek wanted the children to work from their own imaginations and inter-pretations of the stories they were presented with. These children had to produce, in effect, counter-visuals of their own experiences opening up and capturing a different play of imagery invention. It is known that Cizek was reluctant to tell the children what their artwork should look like. He offered advice rather than instruction, and highlighted momentary or accidental realisations as principal actions of art. There were no display of magazine images to copy from, and he showed the children no relevant professional artist's work so that they would interpret the description of stories in visually controlled and narrow ways. However, the art studio in which he once taught in was crammed with children's drawings and maquettes. From photographs of Cizek's art teaching studio, the space around the children was awash with their artefacts, and the experience of our eyes suggests that these items of work were decisive interpretations of their world. This art studio is like no other educational space. Handing over autonomy to the children does not mean that Cizek wanted to avoid teaching. Far from it, because what he had done was to create a different teaching problem for himself.

By not looking outside of themselves to analyse other artworks, the children in Cizek's teaching studio must draw more from their own involved world, their emotional understanding and turmoil that gets them closer to what they want to depict as the mystery of the story they have been set. In this sphere of work the "child has his own handwriting" (Viola, 1936, p. 22) that comes to pass when the eyes wonder, when the child feels uninhibited and when they feel a connection to their immediate subject. To stimulate this 'handwriting' Cizek exhorts that the teacher must listen to the child, discuss with them their work, let them explain what they are doing, and value their own method of painting and achievement in their artwork. There is to be no irreducibility for opening and sharing. Cizek knows how media exploration can stimulate the child's personal 'handwriting', and he also knows why it is important to have on all the walls, and on display tables, children's artwork. Artwork on display can provoke the visible out of children; it suggests how they are seeing things, demonstrates their compassion, and shows to us what the visible can accomplish in depth. The display of children's artwork can bring us closer together by making us keener and more alert. In the process we become more attentive of how children experience the world, and of the poetic power they possess. Each work of art by the child may expand our vision of the world, when each work of art seizes upon a gesture or an energetic movement that advances to explore the depth and diversity of a child's full life. Not to leave it at that, Cizek insists that the children are to have regular ongoing discussions about the visual world of image making and appearances in art. It is an opportunity to hear the children speak about their experiences, to see what they have constructed, to listen to the things that have impregnated their powers to see and how they have represented their meanings. By drawing further attention to the organisation, direction, intentions, recognition, composition, form, imagination, appreciation, and other developmental issues that arise in such discussions, the children themselves were learning how to articulate the language of art while sharpening their perceptions, emotional attitude, and expressive skills.

The slightest thing, however vague, as Cizek acknowledges, can make way for something magical to appear. What is hidden from view may be the very ground that needs protecting and watering in order for a child's vision to occur. It is not an *ex nihilo* experience that produces this effect but serious work involvement. In an exercise like this all kinds of unusual things can happen by chance, accident, and surprise. Cizek, like Collingwood, thought that "expression is an activity of which there is no technique" (Collingwood, 1958, p.111). Techniques and processes are endowed with, and transformed by, the mettle of a free enquiry. Those odd conversations and oblique images that children have are the transmitting shapes of art, the movements that colour the world and light it up. Imposingly, for Read and Cizek, children could express themselves through art with the intent of recording the sounds that form on their lips, and shudder through their bodies; what is beyond vacant expression and inert touching.

One reads the children's artwork that is reproduced in *Education Through Art* as affirmations of the most humble kind, perpetuating some of the clearest and closest insights imaginable. The making of a repose whose superior distinctions are in contrast to some of the volubleness of our adult world can come from children. Read understood very clearly that children's artwork defies us, provokes us, and demonstrates to us why we must always reject images of ourselves that are not real. In the "hot house of culture" (Viola, 1936, p.13) and in our debates about high and low art in education our view of children may slip into adult perceptions.

In appearance or in performance, children's artwork can explain irreplaceable things about our human condition and excellence that one would be foolhardy as an adult not to cherish. Read believed as I have tried to indicate, that what education through art could deliver was an education that was tender and anything other than this was for him not education at all. What better way in education is there to experience new visions, a multiplicity of outlook, the plasticity of one's perception, to discard the weariness of life, to reach for the stars, to know others as part of a community, to feel happy, to contemplate beautiful thoughts and feelings, to have courage, to question seriously, to learn to take responsibility and be part of the world that appreciates who you are than through art as the basis of education? "Humanity has lost its dignity; but art has rescued it and preserved it in significant stone" (Schiller, 1982, p.57). As Perry reminds us, "[o]ne suspects that very great educational deprivation can occur from the 'losing' of children at the primary level" (Perry, 1992, p.7).

I have discussed how art education can help to unify and integrate the growth of children in socially, intellectually, and morally important ways. In a world of closed minds, one can only guess why Read is no longer popular. If my analysis of him is at least partly credible, then I think there is every reason not to cringe and cry foul at the suggestion of educating through art. Because, for all the deficiencies that *Education Through Art* has, there is also the incorrigible sense in it of the value of art education. Only an expert mind would have written: "art leads the child out of itself". Aptly, Read remarks: "For we must in these matters, remain as children, and education should have no other aim than to preserve within us some trace of the penetration and the delight of the innocent eye" (Read, 1970, p.111).

As Goodway points out, *Education Through Art* was "an experience that changed the course of his life, the result as he puts it of visiting many schools up and down the UK to see children's art. What had moved him was the gestural and emotional content of the children's art and by the conversations he had with many five-year-olds in regards to their artwork" (Goodway, 1998a, p.188–9). Read was adamant that art education was the basis of a social process enjoined with a life crammed with happiness and splendour. Art education had to recapture more of the child's corporeal existence in the world. His was an unerring conception of how to reshape 'education for freedom'. A penetrative life is often curbed, Read insists, because we fail to benefit from the impulsion of education through art. Human beings are alive in a multiplicity of ways and our education system, he felt, had to address this issue with confidence. For Read art is the decisive feeling that forms our "stable happiness in adult life" (Read, 1944, p. 32). To see this, we have to return to the child's connections with art as the basis of education, to the vigour and exuberance of their effective gentle spirit that can establish future relations in the world.

Read emphasised the doing, configuring, and the announcement of one's own intensely experienced actions, relationships, stories and rhythms. Providing experiences that would not "invade the realms of other lives" (Zaslove, 1998, p.292) in order to subjugate them was his attempt to reinforce what we are in danger of losing, namely an aesthetic culture of expression, of one's own mental life as positive forms of the children's "sympathetic projection of feeling" (Read, 1970, p.89) addressing itself to the world in a "shared mutuality of experience" (Zaslove, 1998, p.292–3) and learning. Suffice to say that if art education had been the basis of education, the results of education would now look very different.

LANGUAGE GAMES AND RULE FOLLOWING

Ludwig Wittgenstein

"When you first begin teaching, you are teaching yourself. I learned a lot that way. You are trying to put into words and explain something that you haven't perhaps thought about before, or hadn't consciously realized" (Moore and Hedgecoe, 1986, p. 96).

Abstract

Teaching presupposes language games and rule following. A portentous point or is it? On first view it can seem trifling to mention that public language games and rule following are common concerns of teaching practice. Wittgenstein's arguments lie, however, in a number of radical and subtle ways that indelibly find their way into a teacher's approach to student learning. This chapter will discuss how in teaching art we exert public language games and rule following and why these things matter.

Introduction

Wittgenstein was born in Vienna 1889 and the only book he published during his lifetime was *Tractatus Logico-Philosophicus* in 1918. The fact that he only published one book, however, may give entirely the wrong impression of someone who led an astonishing life (Monk, 1991). Bertrand Russell thought correctly that *Tractatus Logico-Philosophicus* was "an important event in the philosophical world" (Russell, 2002 p. ix). Soon after his death in 1951 an extraordinary range of language-related notebooks and manuscripts of his were published. These include *Philosophical Investigations, Zettle, Remarks on Colour, The Blue and Brown Books, On Certainty, Culture and Value, Remarks on the Philosophy of Psychology: Volumes I and II,* and *Philosophical Grammar*.

'Forms of life' is how Wittgenstein describes language games and as, P.M.S. Hacker mentions, the "key to our nature is that we are language-using animals. Our language conditions our nature, conditions our understanding of the world and of ourselves, and conditions the institutions we create that constitute the societies in which we live" (Hacker, 2001, p. 59). In this chapter we are going to dig into this remark and relate it to Wittgenstein's public language games and rule-following notions.

What follows is broken down into three sections. The first section will discuss public language games in art education, the second section will examine rule following in art education, and the third section puts to the classroom teaching test the language game of rule following. Admittedly, our discussion is not going to produce anything near a complete picture of Wittgenstein's philosophical work on language use nor how language is comprehensively used in teaching practice. Nevertheless, a considerable amount of attention is paid to public language games and rule following because these are infrequently acknowledged fields in the teaching of art. As we focus on the visual and performing work of children and adults, the role of language games and rule- following scenarios contain much of the artistic culture that transforms forms of life in art education. Our intention is to demonstrate that we can learn plenty from Wittgenstein that is relevant to art teaching. What follows is not a theoretical debate but a practical account concerning the forms of life in language games and rule following we often use in art education.

As Kjell Johannessen remarks, Wittgenstein's "own voice has been heard only to a modest degree" (Johannessen, 2004, p. 11), which begs the question why this is case when his writings are full of questions pertinent for discussion in the teaching of art. The business of teaching is always about meaning and Wittgenstein shows how meaning corresponds to the public language games and the rule following we use, extrapolating, as he does, how the meaning of a word corresponds to its use in the language (Wittgenstein, 1989, Book 1, No. 43, p. 20).

I believe no one has explained the practicality, sophistication and expediency of our language games and rule following better than Wittgenstein. Language games are used to consummate meaning, as Wittgenstein argues, on the practices we as teachers want to convey to our students, affecting the work they generate in art education. In this process we often need to remind ourselves, as Wittgenstein surmised, that language games are a social practice and that "children are brought up to perform *these* actions, to use *these* words as they do so, and to react in *this* way to the words of others" (Wittgenstein, 1989, Book 1, No. 6, p. 4).

I

Language Games

"A picture can depict any reality whose form it has" (Wittgenstein, 2002, Book 2, No. 171, p. 11).

Language games are the "vehicle of thought" (Wittgenstein, 1989, Book 1, No. 329, p. 107), and "what belongs to a language game is a whole culture" (Wittgenstein, 1994, No. 26, p. 8) and way of life. The whole thrust of public language games are to disclose how we share our lives and connect to each other by the public language games we play. It is in these public languages games that we recognise how we can go on and express the world and ourselves in it in a common weal. In public language games the "question is not one of explaining a language-game by means of our experiences, but of noting a language-game" (Wittgenstein, 1989, Book 1, No.655, p 167.). In teaching we "talk, we utter words, and only later get a picture of their life" (Wittgenstein, 1989, Book IIxi, p. 209).

When a student explores a teacher's language game, noting how this language game is being used, this language game is then likely to express its value as part of the student's form of life with their own certainties, questions, and perceptions in it. Language games as forms of life in teaching relate to social practices that rarely stand still, involving inevitably the circumstances, actions, and utterances we deploy when we discuss making, visualising, seeing, showing, justifying, challenging, describing, performing, acknowledging, and expressing in general and specialised ways.

Art teachers use language games when they can perceive what gives in an object or performance, when things are not going to plan and when more information is needed. The language games in which we engage in art education are mostly gestural, expressive, provisional, and dialogical ones, and, as Charles Taylor construes, they consist of embodied understanding rather than pure intellectual-scientific understanding (Taylor, 1997, p. 173). Indeed, Cora Diamond interpolates in relation to Wittgenstein's later works: "[t]he idea that we have not got *Thought* unless we can rewrite the insights as argument in some approved form is a result of a mythology of what is accomplished by argument" (Diamond, 1996, p.9). Stories, images, and performances, as Diamond declares, are every bit a slice of the understanding of life as logical proofs are. I concur with Diamond and Taylor and others too, that these art language games obey what Wittgenstein determined is a social practice; they follow a custom.

It is customary in the language games of teaching art to enthusiastically point out 'yes, that's it', 'carry on', 'do not stop what you are doing', 'this is sensitive work' and 'I like what you are doing here'. When the teacher says, 'yes, that's it and carry on', what are we to suppose? We cannot understand this language game because our vision is being obstructed by the fact that we do not know what is being grasped here. Taken out of context, the words may mean little but in a context they may be the right words to utter. A student may be feeling confused about the language game their teacher is using in class when, for example, they are told that their image making is sensitive. The same teacher has also said to half a dozen other students in the same class exactly the same thing, only their work appears very dissimilar to this student's work. Our student is confused but this is no trivial matter in the language game of art teaching and learning. If we are to help our student overcome their confusion we might consider that one "thing we always do when discussing a word is to ask how we were taught it. Doing this on the one hand destroys a variety of misconceptions, on the other hand gives you a primitive language in which the word is used" (Wittgenstein, 1994, No.5, p.1).

Any unfamiliar language game will cause some confusion when first introduced to the class and using a world like sensitivity is a particularly difficult and time-honoured concept in art teaching to expedite because of its range. The student understands what the word sensitivity means in a general sense, but the situation in which the word is now used is troubling for the student. The student cannot see how the teacher is using the word, and this might be because they are failing to see that every "picture has as it were, a frame of its own" (Auerbach, 2003). Our art teacher would explain why this student's artwork was sensitive and would go on from there to explain why the other half a dozen students' artwork in the same class deserved to be classed as sensitive work too. The way they might go about this is by discussing and showing how the individual shape, pattern, rhythm, voice, idea, movement, and playing by each student is still nevertheless being expressed sensitively. Our teacher picks out something in the realm of art practice that is significant about the student's work. The teacher draws attention to the delicacy of the student's drawing and the connections they are trying to get across when they say: 'because', 'tonally this is very different', 'in this instance we see', 'there is a change in the way you appear to be looking at this' (Wittgenstein, 1984, p. 55), and 'have you seen the way Edgar Degas in his painting L'*absinthe* (1876) portrays despair?' This is how such-and-such painterly and musical language games are used expeditiously by the teacher. Appearances and the making of them are discussed from various points of view. The student learns by "a particular way of looking" (Wittgenstein, 1989, Book 1, No. 596, p. 156), hearing, and translating that belongs to the erudition of the language game we are playing. In this language game what is being presented by the teacher as student-sensitive art comes from showing, seeing, and hearing and by the criteria involved, "which governs the use of certain linguistic expressions" (Garver, 1994, p. 181).

Samuel Palmer and John Constable are two fine artists whose landscape paintings are sensitively different from each other. Gustave Coubet's painting L'Eternité (1869) captures a reality that is incomparable to Paul Nash's painting *The Shore* (1923), yet both of these paintings are of the sea shore. George Eliot and Thomas Hardy are two very different 'landscape' writers. Their novels and poems are judged to be sensitive pieces of artwork because of the use of realism in their landscape descriptions. The realism of these descriptions will further be judged in connection to their intentions and connectedly to the craft and technique of their ambitions. What it means to produce a sensitive piece of music, writing, dance, or painterly work will get decided in a cultural way. This cultural way adjudges the character of the student's artwork and the language used by the student and teacher. Language games as cultural social practices in art education affect the performing, written, and physiognomic production of how art is learnt. In the course of showing, describing, and playing, our student over a period of time learns how sensitivity in this instance is being handled in their work, and how in another instance it is being handled in their work from another perspective. This student can learn to see that sensitivity in art education can have a variety of meanings and that these meanings relate to a particular practice and its activity. Hence we "don't start from certain words, but from certain occasions or activities" (Wittgenstein, 1994, No. 6, p. 3) and, more often than not, from meanings with which students are familiar.

If our student is still confused by this process, the teacher might ask, as Diamond does in a different context: What is stopping the student looking, perceiving, and understanding? What is the language game they are playing? Diamond feels that the student's problem may rest in their not looking and in their not practicing the art. Our teacher may ask our student, what is it like for sensitivity to be used in this context and they, the teacher, produce further examples in an attempt to influence the student's judgement. Ineradicably, what is learnt is that sensitivity is in the seeing and in the performance. However, the 'like' the student is producing may not be there in a conventional visual, musical, and poetic manner because our student may have other intentions, there are different media involved, there are different visual, musical, and poetic forms being expressed and the incidents or ideas are different too. These language games of Wittgenstein's are publicly concerned with using a word like 'sensitivity' in relation to a customary social practice in art education that knows how to recognise expressions of sensitivity. In its use our art teacher may be referring to the student artwork aesthetic sense in the picture, what is sympathetically real about it and where they may have "lost the hold of the idea that he has to show things being made to happen and not just say that they have been made to happen" (Diamond, 1996, p.46). Sensitivity in art education has to be performed, described, or displayed, where the evidence of knowing this relates to these reciprocal demands that may have "rendered—the play of his facial expression, his gesture, his voice" (Wittgenstein, 1993, p.89).

No matter what we teach in art we all teach to some extent in a conventional and practical way involving language games constrained by realistic enquiries. 'What is the meaning of this', 'how are we to understand this', 'what is its social practice' and 'how is one to teach this'. The realism implied in these language games invokes the ordinary teaching practice we use to comprehend different situations and perspectives. As Diamond notes, this normal 'grammar' is a necessity that further affects 'our capacities as thinking beings' and is "primarily tied to the sense of life" (Diamond, 1996, p. 10) teaching conscripts. Through the course of this chapter we will explore this matter further. Diamond's notion of the 'realism and realistic spirit' of Wittgenstein's understanding of how the mind operates implies those forms of life indicative of everyday teaching. The natural language that says, what would a student have to know to perform a tap dance, free-jazz dance, or a hip-hop dancing display? What would a student have to know to produce an abstract painting or to write a poem about playing football'? The concept of knowing, Wittgenstein reminds us, is "coupled with that of a language game" (Wittgenstein, 1993a, No. 560, p.74). Language games connect to the forms of life we observe going on in a tap dance, free-jazz, or hip-hop dancing displays. These performances are complete with their concepts of ordinary knowing.

It seems problematic to pronounce "the crucial action is pre-verbal: to be able to allow the first alertness or come-hither, sensed in a blurred or incomplete way, to dilate and approach as a thought or a theme or a phrase" (Heaney, 1979, p. 271). Thus, for our student "even the feeblest painter pictures are the stuff his private world is made of" (Malraux, 1990, p. 278). In the public world of teaching our teacher would ask the student to describe their experience, write it down, produce a sketch of it, or ask them to perform it. If a student says they have a great idea, the response from Wittgenstein would be, 'how do we 'know' this?' The teacher might reply to the student that it is only when you have written your thoughts down, or sang the tune to me, for example, will I be able to agree with you that have a good idea. This student may feel all kinds of things and have all kinds of personal images that seem right to them in their private realm, but in the public social world demonstration is involved.

Our 'crucial actions' are never entirely going to come from 'pre-verbal' inclinations because we also know that our 'crucial actions' become revised and perfected by the accompaniment of a public display of work, by what is seen and heard that relates to the meaning of its 'grammar'. When we draw a figure, write a verse or perform a dance routine the sense of such work is determined by its grammatical capacity. While it is true that teaching and learning in art education perpetually involves working things out in language games where actions take shape which could never have been planned, intended, or preconceived (Hagberg, 1995, p. 84–8). Our response to this must surely be that we have to consider what led the student to look at events differently? What did the student see or hear that made them think or act in other ways? When things are not planned, intended or preconceived what capacity convinces the student they are on to something? What have they 'seen' to suggest that certain possibilities are worth pursuing? Stephen Halliwell espouses in relation to Aristotle's *Poetics* that the production of art must be "outward facing, and locates its subject in general human reality" (Halliwell, 1998, p.60). The point of bringing out the student's private thoughts into the spoken-visual-performance arena in the art class is to encourage a normal practice 'that will give my actions the meaning they have' (Taylor, 1997, p. 174). In teaching, did our student "hear the plaint?" (Wittgenstein, 1989, Book IIxi, p.209). 'Have you thought about this', 'how about changing this to this', 'what if this happens', 'are there other ways of looking at this', 'have you noticed that in this instance', 'surely we can', 'I cannot picture this', 'the way you have described this does not take account of x', 'I am not sure about this because'. There is 'a why' about our discontent, when a teacher states: "you need to sing this octave in a higher key'. In these remarks children are learning the language games that express how improvement, substantiation, justification, and alternative meanings can be stated.

Wittgenstein knows that there can be more than one kind of contribution from our reasoning and actions that can change the effects of the student's art. At one level, we see Wittgenstein stressing the importance of 'anti-essentialist' language games, whose realism takes a departure from the logical characteristic of an argument. Wittgenstein tells us that when he is studying philosophy, he must keep changing his posture in order to see new things (Wittgenstein, 1984, p.27). What does anti-essentialism mean and what is its relevance for teaching art? In *Philosophical Investigations,* Wittgenstein is keen to demonstrate how words can have many different uses and openings that a teacher may encourage in order to instigate new ideas. We can imagine an object looking this way, and we can image the same object looking another way too. We can imagine that if we changed the object's colour our feelings for the object will change to. What we can imagine is tied to our ability to put together images that are naturally conceivable in a practice. When the teacher asks one of the student's in their class how they are seeing a picture in the gallery, for example, their response may reveal that they are not interpreting the picture as the course book tells them to. Wittgenstein often retorts, 'how are we seeing this picture'? The consequence of which may point to a different understanding of the problems or issues involved. "What *reaction* am I interested in? The one that shews that someone takes a bowl for a bowl (and so also the one that shews that he takes a bowl for something else)? Or the one that shews that he observes a change, and yet shews at the same time that nothing has altered in his optical picture" (Wittgenstein, 1990b, No.27, p.8).

Words can be used to imply how the object is to be seen this way, and how the object is to be seen in another way, and what Wittgenstein is signifying by these changes, is that there is "no one thing in common which makes us use the same word for all" (Wittgenstein, 1989, Book 1, No. 65 p. 31) types of language games. A line, as Wittgenstein remarks, can be operated in all kinds of ways to do a variety of tasks, and how we are using it relates to how we are thinking about it. The Chambers Concise Dictionary lists a meagre thirty-eight statements of what a line is supposed to be, but Wittgenstein's interest is concerned in the forms of life that demonstrate what can be said about a line as the real nature of it when we can observe it and share the experience with others. Artists are particularly good at conveying how lines can be used in all sorts of witty, sensual, agitated, elegant, and eventful ways. Lines in a painting can have different meanings according to their position, angle, thickness, length, colour, contrasts, or because of their geometrical and expressive styles. Lines in a drawing come together to advance and to suggest something about the student's artwork that he or she has articulated in visible ways. Wittgenstein goes on to claim that what is relevant in one type of language game may not be so relevant in another, and how words are used in one language game can have a different meaning from another language game. Our teacher's use of the word 'sensitivity' when referring to his or her students' work in one class, may have nothing in common with how the same teacher used the word 'sensitivity' in another class less than an hour ago. In one of his memoirs, Wittgenstein writes that "[a]gain and again a use of the word emerges that seems not to be compatible with the concept that other uses have led us to form" (Wittgenstein, 1984, p. 30) remarks "*look* and *see* whether there is anything in common" (Wittgenstein, 1984, p.31). Strategically, therefore, to 'look' and 'see' may change our perspective. Charles Altieri mentions that language "is woven into a context of actions (PI, #7) which constitute the fundamental public norm for assessing statements" (Altieri, 2001, p.240). When language use was studied by Wittgenstein, as David Pears surmises, "as an empirical phenomenon…it immediately became clear that the sense-conditions of moves made within language-games included contingent facts" (Pears, 1988, p. 425). We find Wittgenstein therefore claiming: "Why isn't a saturated colour simply: this, or this, or this or this?—Because we recognise it or determine it in different ways" (Wittgenstein, 1990a, p.19).

Wittgenstein argues that when a student says "now I know how to go on" (Wittgenstein, 1989, Book 1, No. 179, p. 73) we can correctly see whether the student knows how to go on, for example, by observing the student's dance moves. So, knowing 'how to' here, is different from the knowing 'how to' in calculus or biology. The language games are very different in each case. A dancer learns to use their thoughts implicitly and extensively with their bodily movements so that what follows in their dance movements confirms what is right and wrong about how they are thinking and using their bodies in relation to other bodies, the stage set, the accompanying music and the dance drama's possible story. There are physical and conceptual demands. Our dance teacher would discuss other modes of thinking about a particular dance movement. This would involve what to look for and how to express the dance style more suitably. If our student is to 'show' that they understand the phenomena of performance in dance, what kind of performance would our teacher be looking for? What are the reasons for saying the student's performance was good? It is evident in this case, that the student does understand the language game of a certain dance performance because they can show by their actions that they are following a rule, an issue that we will come back to shortly. Following a rule is one way the student can show they understand the phenomena of performance and how its language game is being used. Now, although we can communicate our ideas through "a labyrinth of paths" (Wittgenstein, 1989, Book 1, No. 203, p. 82), each teaching situation will be inviting, determining, following, or calling for a form of life. Wittgenstein argues that one must know how the particular life of the language game we are using, can bring someone else into the same language game to perceive what is real about it. Definitely, however, Wittgenstein also exhorts how easily the rules of conduct and principles in any language game may become so intolerant of other forms of life that its own practice now survives only through dogmatism (Wittgenstein, 1984, p.26).

II

Rule Following in Art Education

Language games are an integral and inseparable element of rule following, and the rule-governing nature of our language games affects student learning. Wittgenstein opines that math education may be seen as following a rule which "is best described as being like a garden path in which you are trained to walk, and which is convenient. You are taught arithmetic by a process of training, and this becomes one of the paths in which you walk" (Ambrose, 2001, p.155). Substitute art education in place of arithmetic and the verity of this statement is not changed. Following a rule in this Wittgensteinian sense relates to how a student is being trained to follow a path. Being trained to follow a path begs the question of whether the path is narrow, wide, overgrown, bumpy, sweet smelling, circular, or pretentious.

When something goes wrong or right in art education we may sometimes look to its rule. "How do the rules enter into playing this game" in art education (Ambrose, 2001, p. 3)? A simple reply is that the rules enter into playing this game when they serve a purpose and seen as useful. An abundance of rules are taught in art education. Some of the more overt kinds are harmony, rhyme, rhythm, verse, scale, or ballet steps. If you want to make a dovetail wood joint, weld metal, use a lathe, stretch a canvas, look after your paint brushes, produce a mobile, make a kite fly, draw a figure in space knowing about picture-plane geometry, print a photographic image, use a camera, turn and glaze a bowl, play the trumpet, stitch and sow, silk-screen a design on fabric, make a film, write an essay, or pass an examination, what must you do? In each instance, "[c]hildren are inducted into a culture, are taught the meanings which constitute it, partly through inculcating the appropriate habitus" (Taylor, 1997, p. 178). In the overt rules that children follow in art education there is always the danger that we may "miss the entire interplay between action under uncertainty and varying degrees of phronetic insight, on one hand, and the norms and rules that animate this action, on the other. The map gives only half the story; to make it decisive is to distort the whole process" (Taylor, 1997, p. 178). For Taylor, a mark, characteristic of the rules usefulness, is maintained by the student's discourse with it.

We know that different artistic cultures have devised different systems for representing certain things, each of which imply that rules have to be followed in order to show the tradition and create meaning. In a complex art tradition, such as those of the Maori or the Haida, all manner of purpose, iconography, ideality, history, geography, status, myth to reality, the living to the dead, ritual and technical knowledge will regulate the activity of a sculptor in these communities. Artistic expression here follows community rules relating to the kind of 'grammar' that identifies what the requirements of the art are to be. When a furniture maker produces a chair for batch production, they will do so in accordance with a fixed pattern controlling the production. A fashion, product, graphic, and transport designer, a filmmaker, and an architect will all follow certain rules in the making of their art.

Rule following can never be "whatever is going to seem right to me is right" (Wittgenstein, 1989, Book 1, No. 258, p. 92). This is because rule following invokes a content whose meaning is real and relevant. Following a rule implies knowing the requirements that are built into it. Yet, to claim that 'whatever is going to seem right to me is right' is just too personal a way for 'knowing' something, if one knows it at all. A teacher could not utilise 'whatever is going to seem right to me is right' as a rule, because there is insufficient information of what things reliably should look like here to be publicly used when knowledge production and understanding are required. As Diamond suggests, there is a loss of the sense of the real when we do not pay attention to the way things actually work and what they are like.

Are there problems with a rule when we add 'and' and 'or' into the rule (Ambrose, 2001, p. 11)? When teaching a rule such as how to make a mobile, the 'art' of mobile making would be a pressing concern. Making a mobile is conditional on how "all the rules together give the meaning" (Ambrose, 2001, p.3) to it. Also, to teach a rule about how to make a mobile suggests that there are other ways of making a mobile. If we show the students various individual examples of mobiles, no one particular example of a mobile in this collection of work is necessarily more rule-governed than any other displayed mobile. The language game we use in teaching art fixes what makes sense of the art of a mobile-making exercise so that it can be this, this and this. In making a mobile, some of its rules may be more flexible than others. For example, the size of the mobile and the materials used may be non-negotiable straightforward aspects of the rule. But, if this mobile also had to express the 'beauty of movement' in its design, the visual styles of this mobile from each student would differ enormously. How can we know that the mobile has this quality? Our response would be to examine the qualities the student's mobile espouses that would lead us to believe that the 'beauty of movement' is a commanding feature of their object.

In teaching art we discuss with students "what constitutes going on in a particular way in terms of communal agreement" (Diamond, 1996, p. 67). A music teacher, for example, will demonstrate to a thirteen-year-old student a number of ways of using their fingers to help them perform *Scarborough Fair* on the guitar. Words, phrases, and actions will describe musically the idea the teacher has in mind in how to play *Scarborough Fair* on the guitar. Consequently, they will say to the student, 'you need to put your thumb in the middle of the guitar neck when playing this piece of music as it will help to keep your fingers in line and makes them firmer'. Following the rules implies that the student position their thumb and fingers as suggested by the teacher.

Wittgenstein remarks: "It is misleading to say that a rule is a statement, a statement about a mark, for then there is a temptation to say it states that we in our society use a sign in such-and-such a way" (Ambrose, 2001, p. 153). If we think of a rule as a statement, "this draws our attention to a different kind of question: Are they true or false?" (Ambrose, 2001, p. 154). Furthermore, in a dictionary definition of what a rule is, how much of it is essential to the rule's ruling in the language game form of life that we are using? "If I am a professor of logic and say a rule is something general or that for a rule generality is required, I am just making an ass of myself. For do you know any better how to use a rule from this explanation? It is quite useless; it tells you nothing" (Ambrose, 2001, p. 155). So one conclusion we can draw, and there are quite a few, is that we must look at the rule's particular use and judge from that whether we can follow it. Rule use determines the nature of the rule and what we can do with it.

Teaching art is a creative practice and rules are invented by the student as much as they are given out to be followed. What students pursue for themselves, nevertheless, has to follow a rule. Their performances must be recognised as part of an acceptable social practice. A student working independently will still have to present their work in a certain kind of manner to show that they are meeting the assignment requirements. The dialogical discussions the student and teacher have together are dependent upon how both of them are listening and using what evidence there is in the student's work to show that they are working within an intelligible social practice of an art form. They might discuss, for instance, the arrangement of colours and shapes, the use of metaphor, the description of a person, or the positioning of their dance moves on the stage. The student has to assure the teacher verbally perhaps while working independently that what they are accomplishing is within acceptable parameters and they do this by showing they are following a rule. The teacher looks to the rule following to reassure the student and to assess their work. For example, how would we know that our student is "seeing the figure as a wire frame" (Wittgenstein, 1990, Vol. 1, No. 12, p. 4) and not something else? Following the rule tells the student a number of things about the meaning of what counts in the language game with reference to how something should *look like* and be performed. Following a rule means that "one has to *look* at its use and learn from that" (Wittgenstein, 1989, Book 1, No.340, p. 109). The accuracy of the rule following for the student must relate to the social practice of the art. Thus, what the artwork *looks like* is tied to a performance that incorporates a culture that lends meaning to it. Rendered as the student's artwork is, its language game may exist "only in the practices it animates, and does not require and may not have any express formulation" (Taylor, 1997, p.178). This is particularly so when thought is engagingly dynamic, intense, and immediate, seeing what gives in the visible itself without exterior understanding in advance. The image of the artist working intuitively is well founded and many a painter, sculptor, dancer, musician, designer, actor, and writer will on this impulse start to write, dance, compose or paint. Equally, we may say to the student: "I don't want you to look at it like that... Where does it lead you to?" (Wittgenstein, 1994, S.3, No. 35, p.27).

It is possible to recognise the rule the student has followed but not the art in it. It is also possible to follow a rule in art education but, because of the condition of the rule, the student's work lacks art. Unfamiliarity with how a rule can be followed and used artistically will inevitably affect students' performances. If a student unconsciously follows a rule, will any art be achieved? What are the steps that a teacher can take to ensure that the rule leads to an art of the rule? We could be at risk here of thinking that the rule is an art, when we should be thinking that rules must serve the art. Then, it is germane to note that we have rules in art in order to facilitate art practice, not hinder it. This might lead us to think there is a break between the rule and the art that has to be bridged by the student, but how is this achieved? Suppose one says in response that the answer to this perceived gap between the rule and the art requires a creative act and the creative act cannot be predetermined and is unconventional.

Surely, we would be mistaken if we thought, 'I now have the rule and all I now need to do is to just add the art to it'? As teachers we can think of the rule as the scaffolding of the art. To see the rule as one thing and art as another, however, is to confuse the fact that rules are part of the ascending aspect of making art; where the art determines the rule and manifests it. The rule is part of the art, so to think that there is gap in this way between the rule and the art is a fallacy. We do certain things with the rule that relates to a social practice that embodies the art in it. One student may say my art is aesthetic and another student may say that my art is conceptual. We could further divide the functioning of a rule by classifying the art as classical, romantic, baroque, or minimalist. Furthermore, the teacher may say the intention of this exercise is to learn to play this ballad or write a poem about the playground. This would be followed by questions, explanations, instructions, requirements, descriptions, examples, and a process. The rules are not art but their use becomes art via their application. The student writes, dances, sings, acts and paints with the rules in mind. Knowing the rules of verse is not art but it becomes art through its use. Unless we know how we can utilise the concept *romanticism* in art we will not know its rule. So, by using this thought in this way in a poem the student has described its art and constructed its rule. One can say, 'I can see that the rule for this drawing is perspective' but this is not an explanation that describes its art and correspondingly how to follow its rule. Only a student can make following a rule an art by using their own perceptions, thoughts, experiences, and imagination. We need rules in art education that facilitate the growth of the student. Any rule-following exercise in art education must incite art production, but it can only do that by showing how creativity is introduced into it. Wittgenstein states that if "I hadn't learnt the rules, I wouldn't be able to make the aesthetic judgement. In learning the rules you get a more and more refined judgement. Learning the rules actually changes your judgement. (Although, if you haven't learnt harmony and haven't a good ear, you may nevertheless detect any disharmony in a sequence of chords.)" (Wittgenstein, 1994, S.3, No.15, p. 5).

The teacher may have an art lesson designed to teach only a rule and not its art. This is reasonable when the aim is to teach a technique like pointillism, how to produce a silk-screen print, or how to write a sentence with a 'simple' alliteration like *baa baa black sheep*. However, in knowing how to use pointillism, silk screen techniques, or alliteration, the students can create a certain kind of art. *Baa baa black sheep* is quite a sophisticated string of words and owes as much to the notion of alliteration as to the creative mind of the person who put these words together. One can teach all kinds of processes free of any art. Our teacher can listen and look at the student's artwork to see if a technique has been mastered and nothing else. If we were to ask whether writing a metaphor means applying its rule, we would all agree on this, but we would also want to know when writing is a metaphor an art and we might respond, 'what kind of language game are we playing?' We know as teachers that one can write a metaphor coarsely without destroying the fact that it is a metaphor. Likewise, the mere act of painting something does not mean that we think of it as art or that leaping across the stage is necessarily construed as dancing, any more than writing an essay is an art, unless, of course, it is written well. What would be the rule for a 'well written essay'? Writing a scientific essay well has an art to it but no one in science is that interested in a science essay's aesthetic content. Delightful expression in free verse is the last thing one wants to see in a science essay. Writing a science essay is governed by science not art. The rules are different.

As teachers we are not only interested in knowing how rules operate, we are also want to understand their relevance but we cannot separate knowing the relevance of any rule from how it operates. Although we may see the relevance of a rule independent of how it operates, in teaching we have to know how a rule functions and have recourse to it, the understanding of which affects the relevance of a rule and can help to describe how to follow a rule. It is arguable that we do not know the rule unless we know how to manage it in teaching. For example, knowing why it is useful for students to learn alliteration in an English class one would refer to its consonant groups and vowels, its form of verse, the affect of adjacent words, its metre, the idea behind it, and its noticeable sounds which we use to reinforce its meaning and rhythm. There are different alliteration traditions in English, Germanic, and Celtic poetry that could usefully be employed. Furthermore, our teacher emphasises its repetition and how it can imitate the characteristics of the 'object' described, how words connect up, how it is fun, memorable, insightful, creative, simple, and complicated. These occurrences arouse the question "what does it mean to understand a picture, a drawing? Here too there is understanding and failure to understand" (Wittgenstein, 1989, Book 1, No. 526, p. 143).

Learning to play a musical instrument will involve following many rules. When music is written down it consists of individual notes, note sequences, tempo, melody, and rhythm. It has a key signature, treble or bass clef, bars and time. Conformity at one level exists and following the music can be read like a car manual or as a racy novel. Concentration and interpretation is required given the complexity of the music score: its slow and fast pace, its changes from major to minor keys, moving your fingers, the position of notes, the melody of the music, and how long the notes are to last. A student over time becomes acquainted with various musical sound structures, patterns, and "contexturalism" (Davies, 2005, p.492–4).

Rules do not necessarily impede any art, and in music teaching, for example, following the rules in the sheet music requires tonal and spatial understanding, imagination, and physical interpretation. Improvisation, expression, contexturalism, and subtlety in music playing suggest that that there are rules to be followed from the sheet music and rules to be followed from the playing side. Musical theory may be written down but this does not stop music teachers having debates about how certain music should be played. In teaching music, sequences are taught: sequences in rhythm and note formation. Students learn in the process of their music education to play scales and arpeggio, and when they start to learn to play a piano, for example, they may be taught to focus on keys initially, building up to some 12-tone musical patterns. Based on what we have discussed so far, the music teacher will have ideas about how the sheet music should be played. Expertly they will observe the student playing and in the process of doing this they will determine all manner of things about the student's playing performance: the rules they follow or fail to follow.

With this background in mind, "if a music teacher says a piece should be played this way and plays it, what is he appealing to?" (Wittgenstein, 1994, S.1, No. 11, p.4) The teacher may remark, 'play it like this', as an indication of how the rule is to be followed. They may further compare, 'play it like this', to a different variation to contextualise. The music teacher will know about the student and their prior learning, their achievement in music and what stage musically they are at. One of the problems we are confronted with, which Wittgenstein notes, relates to use of the word 'explain'. How is 'explaining' being used here is at the heart of the issue. The 'musical way', as opposed to a philosophical, mathematical, or theatrical way, involves musical thinking and playing, references to a musical approach whose language game may be asking that it be played like 'this' (Wittgenstein, 1989, Book IIvi, p. 183) , where the 'this' is trying to show that these group of notes should be played in allegro. "'Now you played the passage with a different expression.'-'- now with the same' and it can also be characterised by a word, a gesture, a simile; nevertheless by *this* expression we don't mean something that can appear in a different connection'" (Wittgenstein, 1993, Vol. 2, p. 3).

How does the student recognise what needs to be produced in their musical performance? Wittgenstein acknowledges recognition as a problem and points out that "'what you are saying, then, comes to this: a new insight—intuition—is needed at every step to carry out the order '+n' correctly'" (Wittgenstein, 1989, Book 1, No. 186, p. 75). The intuition is correct if it "accords with the order—as it is *meant*" to be played (Wittgenstein, 1989, Book 1, No. 186, p. 75). Intuition is the spark. This kind of recognition, however intuitive it is, still requires rational thought, feeling, the intentional movement of one's hands while playing the music to trigger a new intuitive insight that says, 'I have got it'. Does intuition come first or is the case that the student knows how to *look* for things, knows how to make things happen, and knows what constitutes playing the musical instrument in the correct way when they hear themselves instrumentally playing *Scarborough Fair*, that this experience is the more decisive and assertive action? Our student may have trouble with his or her chord playing but the teacher is on hand to show them how the music should be played and heard, and how to make progress with it. This teacher introduces the student to the language game of music and with it directs their senses to everything about it. The student who is learning to play a particular range of notes does so by cavorting, controlling, and directing their intuitive impulses to respond to and focus on the musical score.

We know the intuition is correct, as Wittgenstein states, when it accords with the musical score. How the student played a certain musical sequence is "not something that can be separated from the passage" (Wittgenstein, 1989, Book IIvi, p. 183) and correspondingly the intuition I have, if it is correct, has to come from this receiving. Intuition, Wittgenstein goes on to say, is a product of the steps our students take musically. The steps are explained by following the rule which indicates the next move in relation to tempo, rhythm, or melody, for example. Intuition makes no sense at all if it is independent of musical training and understanding. It is arguable that one does not have an intuition unless it is a musical intuition and how do you get that? Rule following helps the student to know how the work is to be played, to know its technicality and when the teacher demonstrates how this technicality determines expressively its musical meaning, they do so by following the rules that confirm this fact. We derive meaning from the description and use of a rule. However, we are taught in art that the life of the rule is a triumph of what the student breathes into it. The student is guided by this. Meaning is acquired, nevertheless, by familiarising oneself with certain problems that relate to seeing *this*, doing *this* and reciprocally being able to demonstrate successfully how the whole musical performance operates. Students learn to import meanings from language games that can recognise what a musical score is showing and how to play it. Hence, for Wittgenstein, following a rule in art education means understanding its language game. Our student demonstrates this by applying its use with *this* movement, gesture, tone, beat, change, and expression in their work. Often, as Wittgenstein mentions, learning the musical score requires the student to engage in possibilities. "It is just that this expression suggests itself to us. As the result of the crossing of different pictures" (Wittgenstein, 1989, Book IIx, No. 191, p. 77). There is no model of how to do this because one has to personally picture things and their meanings invariably for oneself. Put another way, "[n]o one can think a thought for me in the way no one can don my hat for me" (Wittgenstein, 1984, p. 2).

A mainstay of teaching music, like any other art form, is that "in conversation on aesthetic matters we use the words: 'You have to see it like this, this is how it is meant'; 'When you see it like *this,* you see where it goes wrong'; 'You have to hear this bar as an introduction'; 'You must hear it in this key'; 'You must phrase it like *this*' (which can refer to hearing as well as to playing)" (Wittgenstein, 1989, Book IIxi, p. 202). Our student learns to put two and two together to get four. Even in freer and more autonomous art production pieces our students still have to submit themselves to language games which are congruent with knowing. When there is difficulty with the language game and rule following, we have to "get down to the application" (Wittgenstein, 1989, Book IIxi, p. 201) and "discuss all that can be meant by description of what is seen" (Wittgenstein, 1989, Book IIxi, p. 200) and performed. There are always situations when an art teacher has to look for things in the students' artwork which can alter their position, where a drawing, for example, cannot be taken to be *this* but something else, its understanding lies in a different way when "it looks as if there were no room for such a form between other ones you have to look for it in another dimension. If there is no room here, there *is* room in another dimension" (Wittgenstein, 1989, Book IIxi, p. 200).

III

Teaching Colour Theory and Practice in an Art Class: How to Follow the Rule.

In teaching colour theory and practice one might start off with a *colour wheel* to begin to explain what primary, secondary, and tertiary colours are. One of the exercises the teacher has prepared for the students to practice is how to mix the colours blue and yellow together in their palettes to produce the colour green. This simple rule theory that I am going to investigate concerns the application of primary, secondary, and tertiary colours. It could be reasonably asserted that I have now introduced three simple rules relating to primary, secondary, and tertiary colour theory. The use of each rule can have varying degrees of complexity depending on the kind of practice the teacher has in mind. My purpose is to examine how in teaching we might deploy a simple colour-theory rule that can be expanded in all sorts of practical ways. Although our rule is simple enough, it is anything but simple in its use. The complex nature of colour theory is discussed extensively in Wittgenstein's work, *Remarks on Colour.* We will be exploring some of the learning issues that correspond to basic colour rules in order to demonstrate the language game of rule following that is common to teaching in the arts. An initial issue to think about in colour-theory practice, or for that matter in drama, dance, poetry, or music, is how many language games are there when "we think with a pencil on a piece of paper" (Wittgenstein, 1993b, p.7).

In one of their early handouts to students our teacher defined a primary colour as a colour which cannot be made by the mixing of any other colour. So, before we even get started, our teacher has introduced an aspect of colour-rule theory and correspondingly the language game itself has begun with this formulation. To know this rule in an embodied way we might ask our student to demonstrate its use by letting them test it out. However, a student could not test this theory out unless they already knew what is and what is not a primary colour.

A student in the class asks what is red, and the teacher would reply by pointing to the red in the colour wheel saying that *this* is red, *this* is yellow, and *this* is blue as a way to contrast the colours, but "our ability to explain the meanings of these words goes no further" at this point (Wittgenstein, 1990a, No. 68, p. 11). Let us assume that our students have acquired an understanding of the word 'red' and the way they have partly learnt it has been through a teaching process that has required them to *see* it, point to it, compare it, paint it, and call out its name common with our understanding of 'red'. At this point other kinds of teaching problems may start to appear as the student understanding of red as a colour concept explores seeing it, pointing to it, comparing it, and painting it. All four of these processes may reveal an "indeterminateness in the concept of colour or again in that of sameness of colour" (Wittgenstein, 1990a, No. 17, p. 4). Thus, how many different reds can we see, point to, and paint? Conversely, being able to paint and point to many different shades of red in the world is one of the ways in art our student learns to acquires a significant understanding of red and redness.

Being able to identify a red, yellow, or blue is probably one of the first language games we explore as children but the young child learns to accept these notions without too much difficulty. One reason for this is that we all learn what a 'red' is in connection with the use of the word 'red' with our perception of it and in accordance with a cultural tradition. If someone paints a black square and claims it to be a red colour we might respond by saying that they are either colour blind or they are not familiar with our common perception of a red colour. All kinds of painterly difficulties in teaching will occur if a student is not familiar with our common understanding of colour use. "We speak of a "'dark red light', but not of a 'black-red light'" (Wittgenstein, 1990a, No. 227, p. 47) and "We speak of the 'color of gold' and do not mean yellow" (Wittgenstein, 1990a, No. 33, p. 7). "There is gold paint, but Rembrandt didn't use it to paint a gold helmet" (Wittgenstein, 1990a, No. 79, p. 27). What is being learnt in these instances is neither the "physics nor the psychology of color" (Wittgenstein, 1990a, No. 40, p. 7) but their language games and rules.

Our formula is to mix blue and yellow to produce green. The rule is that by mixing blue with yellow one will get green. There is a problem with this that is not immediately apparent. The rule here is precise and practical, yet clearly in another sense theoretical. How can this be the case? We need to look at this as it unfolds to see that although the rule following is true, our student may have technical difficulties which the rule as it stands, fails to explain. Following a rule like this gives us the correct formula but the *mixing* of the two primary colours requires from us that we employ the rule skilfully. So that what is produced from the student expertly matches the shade of green that is in our *colour wheel*. Plainly, the teacher is aware that not any mixing will do because the proportions mixed may produce a bluish-green or a yellowish-green. In a sense our rule following is *this*, *this* and *this*, as Wittgenstein mentions. Getting started in art education means being aware that, as Peters and Marshall point out, what we are doing may imply a "multiplicity of language games" (Peters & Marshall, 1999, p. 169) that can be played. Our teacher has used a *colour wheel* and is currently talking about how the colours yellow and blue produce green but this is not the only way to teach colour theory and practice.

Another student in the class may shout out: 'what kind of green'? Assuming that the teacher and the student agree this is the green they want, the next question is what kind of blue and yellow will produce it? A murky blue and a murky yellow coupled with dirty water or another colour already on the paint brush, and the blue and yellow when mixed together will probably turn out to look like soil. Alternatively, what kind of bluish colour is one using because an ultramarine blue has a reddish undertone and a lemon yellow has a greenish undertone which when mixed will give a muddy green. These are not, however, the kinds of distinctions at this stage the teacher wants to introduce. Pertinently, though, what the student produces is never going to be identical to the green in the *colour wheel*. So the issue is not one of matching precisely such a green, a futile exercise, but understanding how green is produced and what we say is green and greenish as a colour in common parlance.

Other distinctions are worth bearing in mind in the process of mixing colours: a lemon yellow is perceived as a cool yellow (it appears further way) and a cadmium yellow (it appears closer) is a warm yellow. A lemon yellow and a cadmium yellow may be the solution to a particular kind of problem. How we all respond to colour is embedded in the language-game culture and perceptions we use in art to decide what they contain in a particular context. This means that we would discuss their differences, sameness, and specific expressive qualities that rule for us different meanings and uses of them. In what language games, Wittgenstein would ask, would we want to know about lemon yellow and this would naturally be related to our intentions when we might have a visual exercise that explores yellowish colours. Our teacher discusses what yellow may bring to a painting, what we could not do if the pigment yellow did not exist, or in how we can use yellow to help a contrast, harmony, discord, complementary colour, tone, depth, balance, unity, mood, dominant hue, intensity, leading eye, light, accent, or rhythm in a painting or design-motif assignment. In order to understand colour we now find that there are circumstances in which the language games are now becoming more involved and tricky.

At some stage, whole-class teaching will have to give way to individual teaching. This teacher will have to talk to the students on an individual basis about their personal style and mark-making effects they have used in the tones of yellow in their designs. One student might have decided that their use of yellow is not being used as the real colour of the object at all in their exercise but the yellow colour effect, nevertheless, is evoking something of the quality of the object itself. What does this say about colour use in art? In what way does the word 'lemon' affect our perception of lemon yellow as a colour? Is it sour or is it, we imagine, as a lemon tree in some warm Mediterranean vineyard? With older students, we might discuss how yellow is being used in the painting work of Ambrosius Bosschaert the Elder, Van Gogh, Matisse, Barbara Rae, and Patrick Heron.

The student has the green they want in their mixing palette but when it dries on the paper it is no longer the same green. Mixing watercolours to produce green as well as inks or oil pastels to produce green will result in different samples of green colour on the paper. Likewise, a student may mix in correct amounts of their oil paint of blue and yellow to produce the green they want but when added to the painting, the neighbouring colours changes its contrast to something brighter or darker. All this suggests that the convention that explains how a yellow and blue colour can achieve a green is one thing but, in order to know our way around this situation, we have to teach many things about its use.

We obey a rule in art education because "a rule, so far as it interests us, does not act at a distance" (Wittgenstein, 1993b, p.14). By mixing blue and yellow we have found out something about what the rule can and cannot achieve, but the rule does not say the extent to which it has use in practice, it does not depict its complicated picture of life, but we confirm how we are using this rule following in relation to the language games that determine the rule as *this*, *this* and *this*. It is the language games and our cultural practices that decide its usage. Wittgenstein acknowledged that an explanation of how to produce a secondary colour from two primary colours may only lead "to a provisional understanding" (Wittgenstein, 1990a, No. 5, p. 17) of what is involved. We are limited by what we can do by time constraints. The usefulness of mixing two primaries to get a secondary may only dawn on the student when they start to paint a painting from a limited palette. The actions which follow the rule are components of the language game, too. We can test the reliability of our primary-colour formula and we can test whether a student can create secondary colours from primary colours. We can test whether it makes sense to say whether something is blue-green by the language games that can be used to say there is blue-green here. A teacher would probably want to do this in several different ways.

A student entering the first year of school will understand what the word 'see' means but to 'see' is a never-ending process of educational life. They will have been using 'see' in a variety of situations and will have already learnt some of its functions. Understanding the concept of 'seeing' never reaches an ultimate finishing line, a conclusion which says that I now know all there is to know about seeing. The concept of seeing "makes a tangled impression" (Wittgenstein, 1989, Book IIxi, p. 200). "And now look at all that can be meant by 'description of what is seen'" (Wittgenstein, 1989, Book IIxi, p. 198). "What is the criterion of the visual experience?—The criterion? What do you suppose? The presentation of 'what is seen'" (Wittgenstein, 1989, Book IIxi, p. 198).

I learn the rules that accompany the playing on a recorder the notes A, B, and G because it will enable me to do certain things with it like playing the music score for *One Two Buckle My Shoe*. It represents the beginning of my understanding, perhaps, of the complexity and appreciation of music playing and theory. If different arrangements of the notes A, B, and G, are learnt, the student is showing that they are making use of the rules. Referring to various passages in Wittgenstein's *On Certainty*, Peter Winch remarks: "it is a feature of the manner in which we acquire these practices that we do not, as a matter of fact, doubt their reliability" (Winch, 1992, p.230). Consequently, when a music teacher says play the notes A, B, and G 'like this', they are invoking not only a form of life but a social acceptance of how, in this instance, A, B, and G, should be played.

Our discussion has revealed that learning does not take place without exploring the language game of art within a social practice. The student in this process does not have to grasp everything about the rule and its demands in order to start producing something that corresponds to following this rule. Learning is an enquiry and it involves practice. Students need only to be seeing something relating to the rule for the process of rule following to begin, and as we have seen, what the rule demands can be met in a number of different ways. Although the students may be clear about what the rule demands and may know how to recognise the circumstances in which those demands are to be met they may still have no conception of how to make it happen. To do this "a kind of seeing on our part; it is our *acting*, which lies at the bottom of the language-game" (Wittgenstein, 1993a, No. 204, p.28). I can only apprehend a rule by showing in art education my perspective of it which I exhibit by example and I can only do that if I am embedded in its grammar. In teaching art, our teacher invites the students to cross the threshold of the rule, daring them by any means possible to make the rule following come alive through art. The rule emerges through the art via those vis-à-vis dusted encounters the students has with it.

According to A.C. Grayling, in a community our "practice trainee rule-followers are coached to act in ways conforming with the ways others in their community act, there being nothing to rule-following than the conformity arrived at" (Grayling, 1992, p.67). We should object to Grayling implying that rule following is nothing other than 'conformity arrived at' because Wittgenstein never says this in this way. "Anything that I might reach by climbing a ladder does not interest me" (Wittgenstein, 1984, p.7). "Ask yourself: How does one *lead* anyone to comprehension of a poem or of a theme? The answer to this tells us how meaning is explained here" (Wittgenstein, 1989, Book 1, No.533, p. 144). Rule following in art education is not striving for conformity itself but rather how I know that the learning has the form that is representative of meaning and understanding. Our example of mixing two primary colours to produce a secondary colour was not designed by the teacher as an exercise in conformity but 'what can I do with this', 'how can I apply it', 'what does it teach me', 'what can I now recognise', 'have I tested it', 'have my doubts and questions been answered', 'has the theory proved itself", 'have I been deceived here', 'have I learnt to judge things for myself here', and 'have I been surprised by what I have been able to achieve'? "If I don't know *that*, how do I know if my words mean what I believe they mean?" (Wittgenstein, 1993a, No.506, p.66). The rule following that children learn in art education is designed to be consistent with the actions and reasoning we all use in familiar art language games. It is a process that entails thinking of the language game practice and because it is art education we are discussing we cannot ignore that "one must see what one is looking for in the expression and in the feeling it gives one" (Wittgenstein, 1993a, No.601, p.79). Uniqueness in conformity is the art education way. In anti-essentialist ways and because art practice in education teaches that things can be *this*, *this* and *this*, it is not compliance that art in education is seeking but agreement through understanding in its use. Wittgenstein constantly reminds us that language games can be handles that open doors. When a student finds a rule useful their feelings for it may arouse not only admiration for what the rule can do; he or she in the process may have developed their own creative use for it. They may see the rule's uses in richer and more varied ways. Deeply fascinated by what the rules seems capable of fulfilling, our student reaching upward in thought wants to know more about its possibilities. "Counterpoint might present an extraordinarily difficult problem for a composer; the problem namely: what attitude should I, given my propensities, adopt to counterpoint? He may have hit upon a conventionally acceptable attitude and yet still feel that it is not properly his. That it is not clear what counterpoint ought to mean to him. I was thinking of Schubert in this connection; of his wanting to take lessons in counterpoint right at the end of his life. I think his aim may have been not so much just learning more counterpoint as determining where he stood in relation to it" (Wittgenstein, 1984, p.40).

Conventions are ineffective for teaching purposes unless the student is questioning them, being absorbed and 'struggling with language', and as Wittgenstein further suggests, finding a way that will make a convention in art the student's own vision. In *Culture and Value* he intimates that art education requires an opening out of the student's nature and the illumination of meaning through following a rule in "supple" ways. Examples of this approach are: (1) "'Oh bosh, the lips were parted 1/1000th of an inch too much. Does it matter?' 'Yes'. 'Then it is because of certain consequences'. But not only that: the reaction is different" (Wittgenstein, 1994, S.IV, No.5, p. 31). (2) If the work of art appears tender, it does so, argues Wittgenstein, as a consequence of its expression. Yet, as he further surmises it, expression is not explained by reference to a paradigm because there are countless ways a work of art can be expressive" (Wittgenstein, 1984, p.82). We look, for example, to understand the artwork's physical features, its precise psychological situation. Crucial in the language games we play and the rules we follow in the teaching of art are the aesthetic descriptions we use to convey different forms of life. Like the accentuated and delicately painted lips on the portrait's face, side on, parted, and forced outwards as if surprised by a remark or an event we can only imagine but whose hidden meaning approaches certainty when the painting is more broadly and subtlety studied in the round.

To make sense of art education and to determine the meaning of its gestures is to note the kind of language games and rule following Wittgenstein saw as a way of "working on oneself", "on one's way of seeing things" (Wittgenstein, 1984, p.16), "an act to make oneself known" (Peters, 2000). Thus, language games and rule following in art educational practice do not depend on making everything appear the same. Rule following and language games help to determine meaning in art education, as explained, by their use. The distinctions the teacher and student make in language games and rule following are dependent on the concerns of the game they are managing. However, with guidance our student may be changing the convention when it is not possible to use "the old language-game any further" (Wittgenstein, 1993a, No.617, p. 82). The old language game might not be able to alter its character, probe other problems, see other things, interact with students, and notice that social practice has altered. Its grammar may not be suited to new situations of life and may cease to inspire the spirit out of the student.

"I draw your attention to differences and say: 'look how different these differences are!' 'Look what is in common to the different cases'" (Wittgenstein, 1994, No.32, p.10). Two small boys are running but their gait is not the same, their smiles are not the same, their body shapes are not the same, and the light falling on them from the sky is not the same when they move between the trees. A teacher may say to a student: 'the composition is too central', 'make the head bigger', 'change the colour to a darker red in this place here', 'take a closer look at Egon Schiele's life drawings', 'intensify the muscle structure here', 'do the drawing in stages but think of the totality and unity of the work', 'notice how the lines in the drawing seem unsure' and 'add more tone'. These interjects are part of the common language game and rule following of teaching art that as Wittgenstein contends can change a way a student looks at things. The teacher is helping the student to become familiar with the language of art and why we use it. Language games and rule following show what can be achieved when the student is taught how to pay attention to the forms of life that give meaning to their exercise. The art activity that the student engages in results from certain rules about the art which take account of the games essential characteristics.

We have discussed language games and rule following in various settings in an attempt to explain their significance for art education. As firmly remarked, no rule following itself can claim to produce art, but this does not mean that rule following is not a factor that promotes insight in the production of art in education. A student cannot produce art without relying upon some rule which makes the art activity, for example, a portrait of a face. In an English class a student learns to construct a verse or in a life-drawing class how to master the basics of perspective, the student in either case will have acquired a new skill and a different dimension for making further comparisons of rules. When we can follow different ways to express a rule in art we will incite more of the art relating to the use of a rule to extend its form of life. Following a rule and its language games will touch a vital power of an 'object's reality, its contagious sounds, lurking smile and inviting substance. "A picture held us captive. And we could not get outside it, for it lay in our language and language seemed to repeat it to us inexorably" (Wittgenstein, 1989, Book 1, No.115, p. 46). Language games issue forth not only some of the manner and excitement of the child but they form the immutable and inviolable character of all education. As Wittgenstein implied, language games are essential for students' discourse with the world whose intelligible forms of life will affect how they live well.

EXPERIENCE-KNOWLEDGE AND THE MORAL
WORLD OF ART EDUCATION

Louis Arnaud Reid

"Which subjects should be included, which left out, what is the proper 'balance'? And so on. It is here, in the competition of subjects, that the arts tend to be squeezed out" (Reid, 1969, p 287).

Abstract

This chapter examines Louis Arnaud Reid's contribution to arts education. A personal sketch of Reid's work is given in order to bring into the present a current reading of some of his ideas as they relate to experience-knowledge and the moral world of art education. In discussing these issues an attempt is made to show how these ideas have implications for teaching practice in the visual arts.

Introduction

Reid was appointed in 1947 as the first professor of Philosophy in Education in the UK at the Institute of Education, University of London. His appointment was a decisive turning point that paved the way for a line of eminent educational philosophers to follow. Reid became a champion for the arts in education, pioneering its development. He died in 1986. According to Harold Osborne (1986), Peter Abbs (1989), Malcolm Ross (1987) and more recently Maxine Greene (2001), Reid's work was among the very best in arts educational thinking.

There is considerable Kantian influence in Reid's educational writings. I will demonstrate how Immanuel Kant inspires some of the educational thinking of Reid's own writing on art. A not uncommon trait, Reid shows himself unaware at times of Kant's hold on him. One should not be surprised by this since Kant is still regarded today in the philosophy of art as seminal. In recent well-received work by Jean-Marie Schaeffer (2000) and Luc Ferry (1993), for instance, Kant's status is once again discerned as exemplary in the history of modern aesthetics. I will attempt to defend in what is to follow, Reid's notion of experience-knowledge and the moral world of art education as common premises whose specific ideas appear to stem from Kantian thought.

I

In much of his professional life, Reid attempted to bring conceptual clarity to how art in education functions. The focus for Reid was always on the activity of art educational production. He saw this production as an active autonomous dialogue of mind and body interrelating, inseparably bound to its own world, its presence as the compelled way to make art. We read in Reid, just as much as we do in Kant, that art practice creates form out of the student's own spirited imagination: "as the animating principle of mind" (Kant, 1992, chapter 49, p. 175). In so far as the student experience is a self-propelled, adjusting, and apprehending mind, their own artistic activity can delimit in art practice the appearance of things, provoking greater self-knowledge and further susceptibility that opens out the independent thought of things in representations. Such importance did Immanuel Kant (1992, chapter 43). place on the free-play between mind and body in art production that he came to the conclusion that this practice would be empty and soulless without it. Distant memories of certain events, remarks spoken, a pattern in a tablecloth, and the visible remembrance of a painting whose image-making suggest to the student other possible ways to paint, to express one's consciousness of the visible could be recalled to subjectively influence the student's artistic representation. This free-play of image power in art practice, which is dependent, he felt, on cognition and sensation impressions, a point that Kant makes repeatedly in the *Critique of Judgement*, affects how a student can estimate in practical ways their artwork's evolving shape. The wealth and breadth of art production that we see in the world is reliant, to some extent, on the constant judgements we make in respect of these experiences. Like Kant, Reid held that art practice in education regularly involved "rational deliberation" (Kant, 1992, chapter 43), whose human skill is fashioned by a personal dialectic and expressive style which emanates from work in progress to affect how each object appears differently.

In his writing on art education Reid was at pains to explain why the experience of art in learning was an absolute priority in teaching the subject. He emphasised the conative, imaginative, and strong imagery of art making in action as the primary knowledge base that makes art what it is. In combining an experiential, phenomenological, and philosophical understanding of art in education his approach went further than bracketing art making in reason alone. Art education fundamentally was, for him, ethical, discursive, intuitive, exploratory, intentional, cultural, involuntary, feeling, affective, and cognitive. Art education was a holistic experience.

Resembling Kant's thinking, a crucial aspect of Reid's writing was his attempt to demonstrate how art experience in education was different from knowledge in general and propositional truths in particular. Although he repeatedly states the importance of knowledge in general and propositional truths in education (Reid 1961, 1969, 1973, 1983, 1989), he saw as Kant did, that art production is incapable of working in this fashion alone because art practice gives rise to and is replete with other forces that radiate significantly from experiences which have to do with immersing ourselves in the world as only we can. Let me therefore discuss the reasons that Reid gives to support this claim.

II

"From the earliest years, [children] look, listen, smell, touch and feel, taste…in other words attend to, and enjoy the presentation of the senses, in all their forms. Unspoiled children naturally do these things but are sometimes inhibited (for various reasons) by adults" (Reid, 1983, p.13). These kinds of experiences, Reid believed, could be undermined by "a strong tendency in our society to see truth as being confined to propositional statements. Such a view is extremely narrow, works both against our common understanding and our use of language and has severely marginalized the arts" (Reid, 1989, p. 12). Artistic truth is not necessarily a propositional formed truth because, (A) "[if] we consider the process of artistic making, we find that the conventional distinction between *knowing* and *making* breaks down". (B) Informed by a realist perspective, "[k]nowing in the conventional sense…is achieved through a constructive or making activity". (C) "These constructions reveal our attempts to apprehend and to come to terms with independent given reality, to discover and adjust to what is already 'there'". (D) Changing the way we look at things involves "discovery but, paradoxically, discovery of what was not literary there before the process of creation began. In one sense the creative activity 'makes' its reality and in the making 'discovers' the new thing made" (Read, 1989, p. 18). What makes art practice human as part of a moral life as a human capacity to be human is indicated in the quotes by Reid here in this paragraph and throughout this chapter generally. This point aside, failure to grasp the providence of Reid's argument from A to D will result in a failure to comprehend the realism of art practice. Perceiving what is real is embedded in our actions, experiences, and perceptions in life which, as Wittgenstein remarks, are part of the public language games, and social practices of the art in question.

The moral perception of art making relies not on any mechanism that attempts to firmly condition the student's engagement but rather on the operations of the student to bring to life an image or idea, a reality that is self-formed and imaginatively expressed from their creative standpoint. This is the compulsory nature of art that Kant defended in his *Critique of Judgement*. Reid insists that the individual "aesthetic quality—of a rose or a picture or a dance—can only be known in direct aesthetic experience, very particular concrete experience, and never by means of an abstract definition" (Reid, 1983, p. 12). The students' aesthetic attention Reid construes as inescapably "for its own sake" (Reid, 1983, p.13). By this he means for the student to find their own way, to explore, and to portray an object by sizing it up for themselves. Thus, a formal condition of art practice appears often as 'for its own sake', one which may constitute a "pictorial event" (Merleau-Ponty, 2004, p. 96). This can cause substantial problems for the art teacher. A 'pictorial event' clings to the concrete but is also connected with everything concerned with the unfolding and surging action of the drawing or painting style itself.

For Reid, aesthetic attention invokes in its wake a feeling which "is an inherent part of the knowledge and understanding of art, which cannot be adequately expressed in impersonal propositional statements" (Reid, 1989, p. 16). Reid describes this idea of feeling and its felt use in art in the following way: "How does the functioning of emotion in art-experience differ from the functioning of emotion in life? Aesthetic emotion in the experience of art tends, like its functioning in life, to action, but to conative action rather than to overt external behaviour. In anger, one may want to hit somebody, in fear, to run away. In art-experience, contrariwise, the conative action is a reinforcement of attention to the work itself. It is *retroactive*" (Reid, 1989, p. 20). In the art-making experience nothing will happen to get things right until there is appropriate emotional engagement in the developing artwork. An emotional filled experience full of sensory vividness breathes life into the artwork and is a controlling factor of it. The immediate note of any living person is emotionally charged with the tremors of their existence, and in the course of art practice this may serve the constant forward motion that influences the art-making process. Unless a drawing feels right the work of art will appear to oneself as less than convincing. Artistic emotions are part and parcel of the student's cognitive, perceptive and physical involvement that in marked ways engenders how to decide a face's form, its emphatic clarity, dramatic gesture, and textural roundness, softness, blankness. These felt responses are an essential element of the student's humanness in art making. Under such influence the quality of the student's artwork can be transformed. The student's feelings and the nature of the artwork which produces it aid the process of creation by inciting recognition, evocation, memory, colouring, and purpose. Their presences reassure and assist the student's states of mind, helping them to feel comfortable and uncomfortable in their artwork. The student's outlook emerges from feelings conditioned by thoughts and sensations. A student learns to flourish on these responses as a natural component of the artwork testing ground, an indication of its value and their training.

Reid writes: "The knowing, the cognitive apprehension, of art is essentially direct, intuitive, experiential, and not as such propositional. It can be called 'experienced knowledge", (Reid, 1989, p. 14). This is an important comment because of what it is attempting to imply. It is worth picking out in Reid's notion of 'experienced knowledge' what he means by intuition in art as this will indicate further why art creation in education is an uneasy intellect. Inexorably what flashes, what catches the eye, what is under one's breath when the student is feverishly and restlessly working away, summons idolatrously the kind of self-creation which indisputably affects how certain things get crafted in the productive state. The claim that Reid is making is that intuition in art animates and confers what appears as self-seeking in the outstretched painting hand of the student, whose movement is being directed by personal interlocked interventions of mind and body. Intuitive experience for Reid is often the impetus to start something off in the art practice in order to administer a motion, an ambition, a deliberation. One might see artistic intuition as a necessary step in the art learning process as tantalisingly close to feeling one's way. This experience comes across as an act of faith, a spontaneous reaction in pursuit of realising elusively what the artwork's image might look like. Yet, this is no aimless inclination since it is contingent on the process of making, building, structuring, surface development; seeing, imagining, mood, and past experience.

The paradox of a free intuitive nature that is ready and prepared to respond to whatever comes its way, however unexpected, is derived from a student's mental aptitude and social world chained and alive to the present historically but operating without a rule scientifically determined for it. Any intuitive progress in the artwork, for Reid, relies fundamentally on the student's character, a sympathetic reverence for imagery and moral guidance.

In his *Critique of Pure Reason* Kant defines intuition in general as direct apprehension, inner sense, a representation, an act constituting a mental event, an act which is derivative from sense-perception and capable of producing images, ideas, or thoughts, a condition of 'I think' (Kant, 1992a, p. 153), a self-consciousness state and a product of apperception. Moreover, in the *Critique of Judgement* he saw the intuitable in art experience as a judgement peculiar to itself, one which is reliant on cognition and sensation. Kant describes the intuitable in art making as alert to and vibrating with aesthetic affection. The cognitive-sensation bond in art experience, for Kant, creates its own synergy, standards of correctness and vivacity whose momentum produces something subjectively knowable for the student creator of art. He construes the intuitable in art practice as nothing like the theoretical determination of an object but rather seems instead part of the agent's own moral reflection-outlook, incorrigible and unavoidable. It is a moral perspective bent on elevation and obligations. We can see this in a number of ways.

Take, for example, the following three artists. Jim Dine: "My life is really a history of observing forms and taking in imagery" (Wiles, Dine and Katz, 2005, p. 9). Francis Bacon: "One possibly gets better at manipulating the marks that have been made by chance, which are the marks that one made quite outside reason" (Sylvester, 1987). And Gerhard Richter: "When I draw—a person, an object—I have to make myself aware of proportion, accuracy, abstraction or distortion and so forth. When I paint from a photograph, conscious thinking is eliminated. I don't know what I am doing. My work is far closer to the informal" (Richter, 1995, p. 31). In these remarks a personal morality is being evoked. In other ways to the moral perspective can appear when the teacher and student make a reference to how innocent, violent, distant, sombre, modest, simple, dynamic, relaxed, delicate, perplexed, precious, gentle, and moving the image appears. Kant took these thoughts when applied in artistic ways as analogous to moral judgements (Kant, 1992, p. 225). On the one hand, the student of art is constantly encouraged by the art teacher to nurture a "a temper of mind" (Kant, 1992 p. 157), which Kant surmises as akin to a moral feeling, and on the other hand the student's aesthetic fidelity he hitherto sees as "the enjoyment of sense to the moral feeling" (Kant, 1992, p. 156).

The student's pleasure and displeasure can affect moments of change in their artwork that are proportionately related to the stirring of their own moral outlook. Jim Dine remarks: "I express what I feel about the objects I draw, and I imbue them with myself" (Wiles et al., 2005, p. 11). In this manner many art experiences thrive on the affections of our intuitable nature-training, the representing moments of our contemplation, something which arouses our passions, deepest concerns, energies, "bodily well-being" (Kant, 1992, p. 197) and life instincts. Kant implies that the "visible expression of moral ideas that govern men inwardly" (Kant, 1992, p.80), such as generosity, politeness, prudence, humility, candour, gentleness, fragility, openness, kindness, courage, and strength can, as signs visible in the human body in the form of actions, become hitherto part of the indispensable student dynamic conditioning a regulative principle of how certain felt imaginative experiences will be performed in a dance and expressed in a painting. The modification of sense and experience that is a factor of art practice in education is patiently a morally good habit, one worthy of distinction as it helps to produce superior perceptions.

The practice in art of letting be, allowing, liberating, giving, sharing, commitment, refusing, appreciating, and confronting preserves a true feeling of the student's morality that affects their creative work. In contrast to propositional truths, Reid contends: "The experiential convictions arising out of the direct intuitions of art are of a wholly different sort. They are very complex intuitive convictions of value, not testable for validity in the same relatively simple ways as in the testing of factual statements, but (as we have insisted) involve the whole person, body and mind working together—cognitive-affective feeling an important factor" (Reid, 1983, p.18). In the artwork of Paula Rega, Cindy Sherman, Barbara Kruger, Tracy Emit, Mona Hatoum, Shirin Neshat, Elisabeth Ohison, or Alexis Rockman, for example, their intuitive approach is influenced by their moral vision of the world. Indeed, declarations of moral validity in many programmes and manifestoes of 20th-century art (Conrads, 1970) are widespread and that in art today (Lucie-Smith, 2002) social and political issues are the leading subject-matter. It is blatantly clear that many current artists are genuinely aware of the salient intellectual and moral dilemmas of our world. So much so that it is arguable that moral issues, rather than a solid aesthetic approach, are significantly influencing presently the higher ground of art practice where the sensibility of complacement, liberality, and caring are once again being challenged. The pursuit of a 'higher standpoint' in this kind of art practice might once more rekindle questions about the utility and instructive content of art.

Reid could still assert, however, like Dewey, that human life still requires a passion which when "[w]e look at the clouds: they are 'lowering', 'threatening'; or the landscape is 'serene', the sunshine 'cheerful'. Jagged outlines are 'harsh', colours 'gay' or 'sombre', the flotsam on the tide floats 'wearily'; leaves 'tremble'. The Grand Canyon is charged with significance of vast emotional depth. The creative visual artist shares in this infinite plenitude of daily sensuous-symbolic significance" (Reid, 1983, p. 17). To derive pleasure from such emergent growth may be looked upon as part of the real life joys of what constitutes delicate visual-moral character. These kinds of judgements, which appear as self-evidently good for the student, form part of their aesthetic-moral training for the world that is around them. Making these estimates presupposes, for Kant (1992, chap. 59), a preparation for pleasure which can enrich ordinary life.

If the arts are one of the antidotes against profane vision, then they are so in part because there is active moral teaching involved, one that says, for example 'look again', is it sufficiently 'like' and is it 'true'? Is the student reacting to what is not right, what are the student's drawing skills concentrating on and does more need to be added or taken away from the drawing? Is there awareness by the student of what is strictly visible face-to-face? Are there constant experiments in perception and are there enticing gestures, an imaginative zeal, the sensation of joy, tension, and a willing mind? Can the student still hold onto their original richness, the work's visual unity and their attentive presence in it through constructive criticism? In the act of creating is the student showing respect, dignity, compassion, sustained experience, and endearment when drawing from life? Are the students working through problems, sympathising, showing splendour, limiting themselves, and findings solutions that stretch their vision? Furthermore, since a great deal of current art is about political and intellectual subject-matter, the content of it tends to spotlight ethical problems and choices. New attitudes towards imagery presuppose that ethical concerns in art are now being perceived in some degree differently. With the emphasis on content, the avant-garde in art today with its moral views of the world are challenging the teaching and curriculum of art. If all this is the case, then what we have here are practicing virtues employed to promote the good in the art-making process by effectively influencing its production.

III

Let me now attempt to put this theory into practice by giving an example of an incomplete but typical teaching situation in a visual studies class. It is not feasible in the example that I am about to give to cover all the issues that I have raised in relation to Reid's experience-knowledge and the moral world of art education. What is described is just one example of it.

In a life-drawing exercise, the teacher notices that a student is having a problem describing the life model. The model's body proportions as they are being worked on appear correct but the drawing at another level has no life of its own and the student feels frustrated. Even in the most mimetic of life-drawing exercises, extensive abstractions of thought and modelling techniques will be required. The teacher knows that it is vital for the student to bring more of themselves into their drawing work but how can the teacher assist the student to accomplish this? An art teacher might want to see from their students that they are employing a variety of drawing techniques to depict anatomical details of the life model. Different kinds of drawing techniques may be needed to model the life model's hands across her abdomen, the curliness of her hair, the arching of her shoulders or the fresh muscles of her neck and arms. The progression of monochromatic tones across the body, the heightened sense of a curved line free from any local gradation and the phenomenon of an enormous or limited range of contrasting marking techniques will capture an atmosphere and cause the drawing to express itself, to evoke a certain life. Equally, the teacher notices that the attribute of cognitive-sensation that implicates and suggests a certain felt quality into the artwork is being conveyed by this student in their evocation of the real volume of the human body. An evocation that the teacher thinks may need to be exaggerated in certain places in order to produce a more striking resemblance of the model. Yet the drawing's real volume of the human body vertically standing in a space surrounded by objects can also suggest to the same teacher that the drawing can be taken forward in other ways. The teacher wonders whether the student could also make better use of their surface texture of the drawing to convey more of the mystery of the model.

The same teacher again comes back to the same drawing at a later stage and suggests to the student that they should speed up or slow down in order to create a new gesture or erase certain contours or localise them more appropriately. Further on in the same drawing the teacher thinks that some slight but significant adjustments might be made and in making these changes the student notices how the character of their drawing is immediately transformed. This teacher is aware that there is a multiplicity of ways in which the memorable, precise, and dominating look of a figure in appearance can get recorded. Here we have a teacher trying to help the student bring certain things into focus.

No two teachers will approach a life-drawing problem in the same way. Each teacher may advise a different course of action for the student to take. The correct advice to give is often a matter of personal judgement and springs from experiences that engage the dynamics of drawing: the gestures that play with light, the heavy marking of the charcoal, the corresponding fragility of the model, and composition boundaries of mass to space. Giving advice always leads to different kinds of finishes and visions but that is to be expected. The advice given by different teachers can be very similar but also very different in kind. Subtle differences in advice can completely change how the student sees their drawing. Two teachers may explain the same point in different ways, resulting in different artworks being produced because the language used by one teacher may signify an approach that stimulates the personal vision of one student more than another student. The teacher may be saying the right things but at the wrong time for this particular student.

The teacher may point to an area in the drawing which needs reworking that the student thinks they can see but does not fully recognise. This is because the morphology involved in the drawing can be formidable to grasp for the student even when they are able to see some part of the problem. Two-dimensional and three-dimensional difficulty may correspond to problems of how to build form on top of form and how to weaken or intensify it, how to record the life model's semi-twisted rotation and how it is that the bright autumnal light is advantageous to some and an obstacle to others in their drawing. When the student's eyes are focusing on their drawing and then consecutively upon the life model, vision can produce an insight that advances the drawing in a plethora of ways. The student who is working from the life model has to operate and work from hundreds of personal glances that can initiate multiple recognitions. Each recognition realised, will help the student articulate what is needed in the drawing. Executing superior changes to their drawn image will require further observation, imagination, memory, and gestural technical susceptibility and transgression that are not reducible to known facts. As they draw, the student's own intuitive experience-knowledge and moral decision making takes effect.

One metaphor used by a member of staff can signify different approaches for the art students to take to encourage different accents, shapes, tones, spaces, and ideas. A metaphor may open up a multitude of image possibilities. It is impossible in art education to count the number of ways one can legitimately interpret an art teacher's remark that the student's life drawing needed more drama or a sense of spectacle. The student eyes are open but they can be afraid of what their own individuality holds. The life model may overwhelm them and upset their perspective. Tactfully the teacher encourages the student to perceive with their own impressions, their own feelings, to make discoveries, to become aware of the signs they have created, to see the life model in a different light, and to translate for themselves the depth of their own openings. Reid, like Kant, knew better than most that when the student starts to draw, the mind could "entertain itself as it is being continually stirred by the variety that strikes the eye" (Kant, 1992, p. 89).

Students have to unlock themselves, assimilate, and record their snapshots, the eye of their compulsion. In a life-drawing class expressiveness is never absent, even with a few gestural marks the presence of things in the student's body is seeing in a certain way. Each mark the student makes resembles a dimension of how they feel about the life model; feelings that connect to the delicate way one is handling the image making that one is after. Each mark, in fact, can take the mind by surprise. The image-making process can be mobile, fluid, and vague. Some images come and go, others stay and the full clarity of the drawing is not realised until the work is completed. Nothing is certain and the unexpected variable happens in ways that can be very suggestive. Each mark the student makes provokes image reactions that may get altered as the work progresses. The student is never conscious of all the marks they make as they have also to take full advantage of the living energy that is passing through them. They cannot be unaffected by this surge of strength, the thrill of the moment, the stimulating joy of touching. Tactile qualities, rhythms, sounds, bodily movement, mistakes, rubbings, the dust of the charcoal, and the beat of an uncompromising range of black and grey tones in the or correct look that the student had to express. I believe this teaching example reinforces Kant's point to a degree that art "has only got a manner (modus), and not a method of teaching (methodus)" (Kant, 1992, p. 226). Yet manner can hide a multitude of sins, one of which, if we are not careful, may get us to think that there is a correct way to proceed and depict. Consequently, the prevailing thought here has been to indicate that the teacher of art should allow as much freedom and "personal apperception" (Merleau-Ponty 1996, p. 63) as is possible in order to assist that play of sensation, imagination, and understanding which organises the drawing into something worthwhile. Each mark in the drawing can disturb a climb up or a climb down, a murderous intent or a secret dream. It is a world full of uncertainty and guidance. However, the point of these kinds of exercises, as we know, is to entice an understanding that helps the student develop a feel for things which makes their artwork come alive as their achievement and differentiation. It would seem bizarre to teach art proper with the theory that there exists a dominate image or style.

I have carved a view of art education that is, to some extent, traditional. Some of the normal operations and conditions of this view I have attempted to explain. Appeals to a tradition in teaching can still be part of the immediacy of life and the discreetness of being that commands some of our deepest affections. The important thing is how open it is and can it still speak to us. In this chapter I have attempted to show, as Reid would have done, how the "qualities of the medium have a continuously modifying effect" (Reid, 1986, p. 15) on the thoughts, actions, and intentions of our students. Figurative exercises are never peripheral to visual art education because the human body is an inexhaustible spirit; a mystery that can never be finalised, a moral necessity of reality and a reference to a subject whose structural arrangements in a drawing emanate time and time again the perceptual spell of being that, as the poet Howard Nemerov remarks, "follows relation out" (Nemerov 2002, p. 450). To claim that figurative work is decadent in art education is not to have noticed how self-deprecating such a remark is. Our lives are always impressed by visions which depict some sensitised imaginary of the human form and factual characteristics of it. The human body is a symbol of all things life enhancing. In such a study, as Reid surmises, "attention to form 'for its own sake' is important because it leads to 'clearer apprehension'" (Read, 1986, p.14). I admit that there is constant need to break away from this kind of art practice in education but even in a painter/sculptor like George Baselitz's, there is the gesture of the raised arm, the bent back, the head cocked to one side which, as finely and imaginatively executed poses, enter into a world of human life which can still be a revelation and a dilemma.

In a limited manner I have demonstrated that when the student works from 'nature' through direct observation, there are always surprises and conundrums. To this end I have explained some of the generative aspect of the student's vision: how the serious, sensitive, uncontainable, unknown, different, awesome, and worldly appearance of the life model will, in some ways, move the direction and content that the student's artworks will follow. Taken in by the visible, the student must nevertheless learn how to reconstruct the constitutive power of the visible as their image of it. They create, as claimed, a fragile human embodiment of the figure, a decisive gesture, from a spectacle emerging through contact. The teacher sets up circumstances and encourages processes where the student can express the motions of their mind and body to give the artwork communicative power, something of the "fiction that signifies great things" (Kemp, 1989, p.142). Operating from a human perspective, the student falls back upon themselves to create in the making their expressed perception of the body before them. In this way they avoid seeing the figure as an object, toy, stylistic exercise, and naïve presence. They walk away from the art class-studio knowing that they have experienced the exceptional as commonly found and praised in art educational teaching.

In my discussions I have highlighted in particular the intuitive and moral content that can affect many art teaching and learning situations. In dealing with a traditional view of pedagogical practice in art the aim here has not been to emphasise a conventional approach but rather to stress what appears as precious values of art practice in education, irrespective of one's concept of it. Reid's works is not unique in this respect but, like many in the profession, his thinking with a Kantian edge to it reaffirms what surely arises in the making of some art. He understood as many have noted how primordially aesthetic our lives are in the world. Remarking, as he does, how personal character, places, events and, moral values are part of our knowledge of the world. I believe that the concerns I have addressed here are critical issues in teaching art that deserve further attention and discussion of them. We need sometimes to remind ourselves that intuitive experiences and moral attention are predicated attributes for solutions in art-making education. They also support the student's life in general by strengthening their mind and body, the free formation of themselves and the elegance, delight, and beauty that will figure in so much of their current and future existence and that of others.

CHAPTER 6

THE INDIVIDUAL VISION

Maurice Merleau-Ponty

"Every visual something, as individual as it is, functions also as a dimension, because it gives itself as the result of a dehiscence of being" (Merleau-Ponty, 2000a, p.187).

Abstract

As out of favour as it may seem to be, we will be analysing why we need a student-centred approach for the teaching of art. This in itself is not a new concept. However, Merleau-Ponty's thesis on this matter is. He tells us something new about the teaching of art that is infectious and of commanding importance. Explained within an art-teaching context is how we might better understand the child's own situation, natural attitude, and lived creative experience to transform teaching in art. In this regard, for Merleau-Ponty, it is the tutelage of the children's surroundings, their personal body-perceptions and the adumbrations of their movements and experiences which, in a unified way, directly affects vision and visibility in art education.

Introduction

Education in art has always trained students to think for themselves but within a process that subjects them to the concerns of others. It has reasoned that the teaching of oneself in art opens up perceptions new. That what strengthens the world and one's own personal existence in it, is in proportion to an individuality energetic enough to have impulses of it's own that add value to life. Human life in art education may seem to encourage, therefore, a richer, diversified, and animated embodiment of a human being. Merleau-Ponty, in this debate, stands out as an important figure. His account, particularly relevant for art education, concerns a 'natural' kind of embodied understanding of the self in art learning experiences. The human body, for Merleau-Ponty, exerts its own feelings, character, and movements to produce an affect that is constantly on hand to calculate the self intimately, and be the steam engine of our thoughts to sometimes correct and complete certain judgements that are needed. Our human body is one of the core principles of intelligent action that guides the self. Educational policies that ignore the sensitive perceptions of the human body are in error of what can affect deeply human predisposition. Merleau-Ponty turns to art practice to demonstrate the value of what the human body can achieve when we are more reliant on this susceptibility.

Merleau-Ponty's philosophical work is one of most challenging and head-turning conceptions on how we should be teaching art. It is provocative and profound. He constructs a phenomenological account of art practice and argues that what reveals art as meaningful in education is the child making themselves understood. In a number of his publications he shows himself to have an explicit interest in the visual arts and children's education. The following discussion will attempt to highlight within a visual arts educational approach that has also implications for teaching in the performance and literary arts, how Merleau-Ponty's philosophy can make a diacritical difference in the teaching of art. Our aim is to reveal in a pedagogical manner how to strengthen the teaching of art. To show this we must verify how Merleau-Ponty phenomenology proves to be useful for teaching.

In 1961, Merleau-Ponty died at the age of fifty-three. "If he had not died so early in this career, there is no doubt that he would have been regarded as the most brilliant of contemporary French philosophers, offering a very challenging and complex account of what he sees as …our embodiment in the world which seems pre-ordained to meet and fulfil our meaning-intending acts" (Moran, 2000, p. 391). This is a commonly held view of Merleau-Ponty, but by and large his writings have rarely been taken seriously in educational policy discussions and his recommendations have been put to the test even more rarely. Are phenomenological studies simply too daunting or unwieldy for education to be taken seriously? Unused, his thinking still represents a formidable wing of thought, so I will argue, for the teaching of art in education.

At the core of his philosophy was his belief that any successful teaching of art owes more to the intricacies of the child's inspection than to "an object-in-general" (Merleau-Ponty, 2000a, p. 159). In *Eye and Mind* and elsewhere, he attempts to show how human life can "[manipulate] things and gives up living in them" (Merleau-Ponty, 2000a, p. 159). When empiricism is successful in one area, he says, its model is then "tried out everywhere else" (Merleau-Ponty, 2000a, p. 160). Everything that enters the laboratory is reduced to "a set of data-collecting techniques" (Merleau-Ponty, 2000a, p. 160) that then constructs a "model of human machines" (Merleau-Ponty, 2000a, p. 160). Immobilised, the human subject is held up with forceps under a microscope (Merleau-Ponty, 2000b, p. 101) "to revoke our consent at each instant" (Merleau-Ponty, 2000b, p.103).

Pedagogically we may find the above remarks problematic but, in defence of Merleau-Ponty, our detachable, minimizing, nominal, predetermined, superimposed, indifferent, and standardised world forgets "experience in its brute state" (Barbaras, 2004, p. xxiv). It is the "slender twig upon which unforeseeable crystallizations will form" (Merleau-Ponty, 2000a, p. 160). Thinking operationally must coexist, Merleau-Ponty held, with forms of teaching that are open to the spontaneity and perspective of the student's life. Already a person capable of sense-experience, self-regulation and with judgement, the student's own situation is an "effective present" (Merleau-Ponty, 2000b, p. 101) with governance. The student is bodily active for Merleau-Ponty and this makes all the difference in the world to the challenges they encounter. Art education in "full innocence" "draws upon the fabric of brute meaning" (Merleau-Ponty, 2000a, p. 161). As bodily perceivers, our students can draw their own attraction, perceptual context, horizon, and understanding of situations. Creative self-transformation in vision and visibility is capable of recapturing as a new object "what is already at work in the spectacle of the world" (Merleau-Ponty, 2000b, p. 45). Insisting, as Merleau-Ponty does, that art education must preserve our "unformulated life" (Merleau-Ponty, 1996, p. 69), the life of an unfolding and transforming being in its primacy, and a life that should be "without impingement" (Merleau-Ponty, 1981, p. 148). Art education should rediscover more of the actual living experience of the student, how things can be reached in a variety of different ways and in the process privilege this experience in teaching and learning.

Thus part of his thesis is the idea that the student's own situation in art education must be construed by how they take their own bodies with them (Merleau-Ponty, 2000a, p. 162). The student takes their body with them because the human body is an "entirely governable body that is, however, set in the midst of initially alien and ungovernable circumstances into which he must introduce order so that they may be liveable and durably endurable" (Todes, 2001, p. 41). How children in art education take their bodies with them affects their vision and visibility. The argument that Merleau-Ponty constructs about this is that art education should "concentrate upon re-achieving a direct and primitive contact with the world" (Merleau-Ponty, 2002, p. vii). He maintains that the focus should be on how the child's immanence should serve as the principle of their authentic expression in art education. The child's immanence and their movement helps to prevent the "sterile reproduction of the visible itself" (Marion, 2004, p.29). The student's living bond with their own bodies summons a way of thinking and seeing for themselves that opens them up to themselves.

Merleau-Ponty never denies the significance of an intellectual inquiry, of strategies, operations and plans, but feels that how we learn in art has one-sidedly forgot the relevance of bodily life, "brute meaning". The child's opening as a "see-er" is simultaneous with their full innocence coming face-to-face with the real world in the learning process. How the child creates their own history in art education led him to believe that we needed to relearn to express life in order to understand it better (Merleau-Ponty, 2002, p. xxiii).

I

Strikingly, what Merleau-Ponty means by teaching children art involves: (1) "Primordial modes of expression for their own sake and as positive accomplishments" (Merleau-Ponty, 1981, p. 149). (2) The child renders their "relation to the world in accordance with what it is under the gaze of an infinite intelligence" (Merleau-Ponty, 1981, p. 150), a body whose human experiences have the capacity to make sense of the world and is the defining subject of it (Todes, 2001, p. 88). Our relation to the world is bodily perceived and this is a key factor for Merleau-Ponty in self-development. (3) Art education should be a practice that leads "us back to a vision of things themselves" (Merleau-Ponty, 2004, p. 93). This implies the child's grasp of the world is "rooted in the perceived world" (Barbaras, 2004, p. xxix) of the child, their experience. (4) An art education that restores the "power to signify, a birth of meaning, or a wild meaning, an expression of experience by experience" (Merleau-Ponty, 2000, p. 179). Hence, the actual working process of art education is to be accomplished freely and receptively. It should stimulate an increase of life by being open to being in the world. Running together, one way of putting these concerns into teaching practice is to consider the following:

"The point is that the aim is no longer to construct an 'objective' emblem of the spectacle or to communicate with whoever looks at the drawing by providing him with the key to the numerical relations true for any and all perceptions of the object. The aim is to leave on the paper a trace of our contact with this object and this spectacle, insofar as they made our gaze and virtually our touch, our ears, our feeling of risk or of destiny or of freedom vibrate. It is a question of leaving a testimony and not any more of providing information" (Merleau-Ponty, 1981, p. 150).

Yet, teaching art must achieve "a more exact vision and a more exact visible" (Merleau-Ponty, 2000, p. 170). To achieve this, the teacher starts from the child's own experience that takes place in a tactile space. In dialogue with the student the teacher explores ways of developing, communicating, and expressing the child's perceptions that render the visible. A teaching practice concerned on the one hand with "delimiting visibility" (Marion, 2004) and on the other with reinstating the child's art as "opening to the thing that is incontestable in visual experience" (Barbaras, 2004). What delimits and reinstates more visibility in teaching art is "the task of seeing what gives itself" (Marion, 2004, p.viiii). There is no vision and visibility, Merleau-Ponty surmises, without touching and being touched by things in the world. What the artwork gives in the visible comes from being immersed in the dimensions of the visual field and being "caught up in things" (Merleau-Ponty, 2000a, p. 163). Probing, my feelings for the world are part of the texture of the thing it attracts. My life is full of incidents where "I have only to see something to know how to reach it and deal with it" (Merleau-Ponty, 2000a, p. 162), argues Merleau-Ponty.

What reassures us of depth, time, perceptual judgement, dexterity, distance, and movement comes from a child's body that sees in visible ways. A seeing that is part of the body's infrastructure that makes things explicit and into an experience. One of Merleau-Ponty's conceptions is that the human body is sensible for itself. The child sees how things are changing in their artwork by looking and can see objects against backgrounds. They can freely develop their own responses to their artwork and they learn to understand something of the other by looking. The student body adjusts itself so that it can pick up individual motifs, stylistic turns and figures in space with ease and foresight, crafting and manipulating objects against different conceptions of life. Children and adults know where they are standing and can move towards places identifying all manner of "spatial features of an object like size, shape and orientation" (Kelly, 2003, p. 64) which, as Sean Kelly goes on to state, have some important consequences for cognition in general, motor intentionality and activity. Our bodies, as Merleau-Ponty declares, "surge towards objects to grasp and perceives them" (Merleau-Ponty, 2002, p. 121) because we exist as "self-moved movers in the world" (Todes, 2001, p.262) where, as Samuel Todes further claims, "our body plays a basic formative role in our making sense of everything" (Todes, 2001, p.263).

The child's vision solves problems and manifests them in its poise. Vision, Merleau-Ponty, Barbaras, Marion, and Todes agree, comes alive in its spontaneous existence, in a unique totality, in the activity that is vision that moves itself and "in the life of the actual" (Merleau-Ponty, 2000a, p. 164). Out of effervesce, students are always engaging the visible in their lives, responding to things in visible ways and as acts emblematic of the visible. Vision and visibility constitute the "centrifugal movement" (Merleau-Ponty, 2000b, p. 48) of the body's acting potential. Through the visible we can make ourselves known and understood.

"The eye sees the world, sees what inadequacies [manques] keep the world from being a painting, sees what keeps a painting from being itself, sees—on the palette—the colours awaited by the painting, and sees, once it is done, the painting that answers to all these inadequacies just as it sees the paintings of others as other answers to other inadequacies" (Merleau-Ponty, 2000a, p. 165).

Putting vision back into education helps makes the world more of what the world really is "part of its full definition" (Merleau-Ponty, 2000a, p. 163), vision as reality and sensitivity of life that "make the world vibrate" (Merleau-Ponty, 2000b, p. 7). Vision, Merleau-Ponty maintains, is a human viewpoint, a component of the child's access to being determined by their own actuality. No art teacher would disagree with his suggestion that the student must learn from seeing (Merleau-Ponty, 2000a, p. 165). A form of teaching that emphatically would insist on vision as "thought in contact" (Merleau-Ponty, 2000a, p. 177), as real life as it presents itself in social self-accounting ways. Art education must not therefore be simply concerned with teaching figurative or abstract painting, for example, but rather be the real performance of seeing itself. One which facilitates the child's vision as a "concentration of coming-to-itself of the visible" (Merleau-Ponty, 2000a, p. 181). In vision the student comes back to themselves (Merleau-Ponty, 2000a, p. 186).

Merleau-Ponty indicates that the teaching of art must return to situations that invoke: "the world [that] is all around me, not in front of me. Light is viewed once more as action at a distance. It is no longer reduced to the action of contact or, in other words, conceived as it might be by those who do not see in it. Vision reassures its fundamental power of showing forth more than itself. And since we are told that a bit of ink suffices to make us see forests and storms, light must have its imaginaire. Light's transcendence is not delegated to a reading mind which deciphers the impacts of the light-thing upon the brain and which could do this quite as well if it had never lived in a body. No more is it a question of speaking of space and light; the question is to make space and light, which are there, speak to us. There is no end to this question, since the vision to which it addresses itself is itself a question. The inquiries we believed closed have been reopened" (Merleau-Ponty, 2000a, p. 178).

II

Practically, how might we try to implement Merleau-Ponty's thinking for art education and what are some of the principal parts of it that might guide the construction of a syllabus and our teaching response? Let us begin by first pointing out as a précis what the teacher would oversee.

- The 'object' (Merleau-Ponty, 1981, p. 148) which the student writes about, paints, designs, or sculpts, can never totally complete our understanding of the 'object' because sense is interrogative, historical and situational. "There are silent signals which come to me from every part" (Merleau-Ponty, 2004, p. 97) of the nature of the material I am working on. What I see reorganizes itself according to new dimensions of it (Lefort, 2000, p. xxi).
- Where to start from in art education should relate to how things present themselves to the student's situation. We "should examine the movement that inclines us to give our adherence to things and to one another" (Lefort, 2000, p. xxiv).
- An exercise is explored from the child-adult's situation that is "caught up in the fabric of the world" (Merleau-Ponty, 2000a, p. 163).
- The child who looks is not foreign to the things he or she looks at.
- The student's whole body perceives, moves, and elucidates.
- The student's experience and perceptions must involve a dialogue with itself, the world, other students, and the teacher.
- Our student takes in different views of the object, incident, or event that is the result of their heightened life.
- Our student is restricted to what they can see and where one can go (Marion, 2004, p. viiii).
- Student perceptions must be rigorous, rather than a leisurely examination of the world. They are part of a teaching process that emphasises clarification, building, exploring, cultivating, adjusting, and culminating activity.
- The immediate, historical, situational, and spontaneous as the essences of brute meaning are fundamental functions of art making and should be in constant use because they are a cause of creative self-transformation.
- The learning process must involve some tradition. For example, some of the rules of anatomy (Merleau-Ponty, 1996, p. 67). Cézanne went to the Louvre everyday when he was in Paris (Merleau-Ponty, 1996, p.67). As a student living in "Florence in 1925, Henry Moore each day paid an early morning visit to the Carmine Chapel before going anywhere else...following the footsteps of Botticelli, Leonardo, Michelangelo, Raphael and Perugino" (Wegner, 1992, p. 1).
- For the student to seek expression and vision through experiencing, habituating, and "going to the heart of things" (Merleau-Ponty, 2000, p. 167) 'by taking their body with them'.
- The student's artwork is a construction and an invention. This construction and invention-making process involves its own "ontogenesis" (Merleau-Ponty, 2000, p. 167).
- A teacher is to create exercises that are designed to extend the visual, invisible, spontaneous, exploratory, surprising, experimental, thoughtful, passionate, sensual,

poetic, playful, and intuitive. To include "world-being, thing-being, imaginary being, and conscious being" (Merleau-Ponty, 2000b, p. 7).
- For the student to learn how to create for themselves "the possibility of a fresh impact" (Bachelard, 1994, p. xxxiii). The teaching of art supports openness, new developments, and the power of making even when what is produced is untrue "by thinking through our errors" (Merleau-Ponty, 2000a, p. 21).
- The use of relevant artistic skills to assist the visible in the vision-making process. To capture, share, objectify, and convey. The student learns to make visible "how the world touches us" (Merleau-Ponty, 1996, p. 70) and how appearances vibrate.
- The student's artwork is to be seen as a celebration of their vision and expressive power.

Before I give some practical examples which Merleau-Ponty's uses to assist teaching practice in art education that corresponds to the above considerations, at least one further issue needs to be raised. Our student production of art in education involves the notion of "invisibility" (Merleau-Ponty, 2000a, p. 187). When Jean-Luc Marion argues that the "invisible provokes the visible in its depth" (Marion, 2004, p.5), he is agreeing with Merleau-Ponty that invisibility installs the visible in art. In Chapter One, we discussed how the photographer Arnold Newman produces the invisible in the visible. How a gesture, a tone, a look, a setting, and an ambiance can 'provoke the visible in its depth' raising it so that we see more of the artwork's perspective, the invisible on the visible. The students' look at the world, but they only become fully alive to the scene when they notice the artwork's qualities, the unsuspected turns that produce new openings. Oversight is common. Newman measures the social feeling and intensity of life in his figures, externalising photographically to a higher degree reasonable associations of some imputed truth. What may often go unseen in art is when we oversimplify how expression works, when we disregard the potency and authority of other sentiments. To extend vision, truth, and reality about the subject matter in a painting involves conversations with certain invisible elements that slowly but surely increase the visible in the work of art. The student's inner impulse which affects the concrete appearance of their artwork contains the passing through and the fulfilment of some invisible commitments that will adjust the character of their work.

The notion of invisibility relates in a practical way to how colours are built up on a canvas, one on top of the other, how we might not see the shadows in the painting as we focus on the main subject of the artwork, how the artwork changes as we move around it, or how the artwork expresses and questions the unthinkable, the disturbing, and the beautiful in the world. The invisible component can be the range of experimental sketched drawings that one does not see in the finished student's work. Each drawing as an experiment is being aroused by other possibilities, backsliding ideas, and reformulations of earlier work in order to further approach the character of what can give in a particular drawing exercise. These experiments represent part of the student's inner struggle and heightened sensibilities towards their subject matter. The student's artwork is changing and developing. Very often in practice the student's painterly lines are constantly being reworked. Invariably, lines get reduced, hardened, or thickened. Instantaneous judgements about the artwork are made that we do not see. There is resistance and concealment from the student in the making of their artwork. Eccentric eye movements and thousands of touches, feelings, and thoughts collide and intertwine in the process of making art. There is the student's first, second, third, fourth, and countless other visible experiences whose exploratory movements in an assignment unite and are bound up with the mark-making effects and sense-date properties in the painting or sculptural exercise. The alterations and changes that are made can reopen new directions and the erasure of marks in the student's artwork and the errors, chances, unforeseen and surprising happenings that do occur, can "pierce in transparency the visible only in order to raise it" (Marion, 2004, p.5). Furthermore, the practical consideration of other points of view which affect the making of the art work is nourished by the student's cooperation with others.

Invisible is how the artwork can show more than itself when recovering perhaps the student's own history. The student's past life influences their present life, but perceptions do change. In an instant, the student's split-second reactions may proceed to give way to a new sensory understanding of the student's subject matter. The constant turning of one's head and the lifting of one's arm that picks up the paintbrush to do something unusual with it are actions essential to the visible. These actions are not contrary to the visible but rather seem to entice, renew, and liaise with what the visible demands for seeing. The invisible is part of the very process which assists the unfastening of space for the student and adds greater depth to the visible in the artwork. This "tour de force" (Merleau-Ponty, 2000b, p. 136) of invisibility can change everything because in a split second such a touch, efficaciously desired and self-determined, may be the aspect the student has been looking for, in a split second there may be recognition, and by turning my head at this particular moment I may notice something that has baffled me for far too long. These actions are cumulative, unobserved, ontogenetic, and determinate. "The painting thus plays between the two extremes of intentionality: the lived experience [*vécus*], perceptions, founded [*éprouvés*] and real, on the one hand, and the aimed-at intentional object seen invisibly and ideally, on the other" (Marion, 2004, p.13).

Having broken down into a précis what the teacher of art might be guided by, some of the examples that Merleau-Ponty gives as instances that penetrate the teaching of art in the visible and the invisible are:

– "We could try not to render our relation to the world, in accordance with what it is under the gaze of an infinite intelligence. Then, at a stroke, the canonical, normal, or 'true' type of expression would no longer be two-dimensional perspective. We would then be liberated from the constraints that perspective imposed upon drawing—free, for example, to express a cube by six squares 'disjoined' and juxtaposed on the paper, free to draw in the two faces of a bobbin and join them by a sort of bent stovepipe, to represent death by transparency in its coffin or the look by two eyes separated from the head, free not to have to mark the 'objective' contours of the alley or of the face and in contrast to indicate the cheek by a circle" (Merleau-Ponty, 1981, p. 150).

Merleau-Ponty is not attempting to undermine two-dimensional perspective. His claim, instead, is that the child's vision should stir how things appear in the artwork as their horizon that bursts forward to impose itself in the artwork-making process. It is the child's sensitive input which makes the exercise come alive, shudder, quiver, and eclipse, without which the result will be a lifeless 'object' bereft of true vision.

- "It is also what Claude Lorrain does when he renders the presence of light through the shadows which surround it and thus more eloquently than could have rendered it by trying to draw the shafts of light" (Merleau-Ponty, 1981, p. 150).
- "As André Marchand says, after Klee: "In the forest I have felt many times over that it was not I who looked at the forest. Some days I felt that the trees were looking at me, were speaking to me...I was there, listening...I think the painter must be penetrated by the universe and not want to penetrate it...I expect to be inwardly submerged, buried. Perhaps I paint to break out" (Merleau-Ponty, 2000a, p. 167).
- From footnote No.15 in *Eye and Mind*: "A minute in the world's life passes! To paint it in its reality! And forget everything for that. To become that minute, be the sensitive plate,...give the image of what we see, forgetting everything that has appeared before our time" (Merleau-Ponty, 2000a, p. 169).
- "Da Vinci's comment that the "secret of the art of drawing is to discover in each object the particular way in which a certain flexuous line, which is, so to speak, its generating axis, is directed through its whole extent" (Merleau-Ponty, 2000a, p. 183).
- "For henceforth...the line no longer imitates the visible; 'it renders visible'" (Merleau-Ponty, 2000a, p. 183).
- There is nothing that should prevent the child "from going back to one of the devices he has shield away from—making it, of course, speak differently. Rouault's contours are not those of Ingres" (Merleau-Ponty, 2000a, p. 188).
- "When through the water's thickness I see the tiling at the bottom of a pool, I do not see it despite the water and the reflections there, I see it through them and because of them. If there were no distortions, no ripples of sunlight, if it were without this flesh that I saw the geometry of the tiles, then I would cease to see it as it is and where it is—which is to say, beyond any identical, specific place" (Merleau-Ponty, 2000a, p. 182).
- "Cups and saucers on a table seen from the side should be elliptical, but Cézanne paints the two ends of the ellipse swollen and expanded" (Merleau-Ponty, 1996, p. 63).
- "In giving up the outline Cézanne was abandoning himself to the chaos of sensation" (Merleau-Ponty, 1996, p. 63).
- "Painting a face 'as an object' is not to strip it of its 'thought'" (Merleau-Ponty, 1996, p. 66).
- "'All through my youth', said Cézanne, 'I wanted to paint that, that tablecloth of fresh-fallen snow'" (Merleau-Ponty, 1996, p. 66).
- We see the depth, the smoothness, the softness, the hardness of objects" (Merleau-Ponty, 1996, p. 65).

- "Each brushstroke must satisfy an infinite number of conditions" (Merleau-Ponty, 1996, p. 65).
- "You draw a woman, but you do not see her" (Merleau-Ponty, 1996, p. 69). "The *thing* is therefore less important than the *qualities of things*, in that they are the origin of all appearances, composing them" (De Whaelhens, 1996, p. 176).
- "Before expression, there is nothing but a vague fever, and only the work itself, completed and understood, will prove that there was something rather than nothing to be found there" (Merleau-Ponty, 1996, p. 69).
- "To capture this envelope of light" (Merleau-Ponty, 1996, p. 61).
- "We live in the midst of man-made objects, among tools, in houses, streets, cities, and most of the time we see them only through the human actions which put them to use. We become used to thinking that all of this exists necessarily and unshakably. Cézanne's painting suspends these habits of thought and reveals the base of inhuman nature upon which man has installed himself. This is why Cézanne's people are strange, as if viewed by a creature of another species" (Merleau-Ponty, 1996, p. 66).
- "Cézanne declared that a picture contains within itself even the smell of the landscape" (Merleau-Ponty, 2002, p. 371).
- There is no possibility of understanding the student's work without looking at it and being stimulated by it.

III

In *Eye and Mind* Merleau-Ponty describes "brute meaning" as rudimentary to art education. In Dewey's critique of *Art as Experience* there are some lines which could have been written by Merleau-Ponty. In particular, to repeat a quote we have used in Chapter 2. "We see without feeling; we hear, but only a second-hand report, second hand because not reinforced by vision. We touch, but the contact remains tangential because it does not fuse with qualities of senses that go below the surface" (Dewey, 1980, p.21). Going below the surface of depersonalisation requires for teaching that the child be "immersed in the visible by his body, itself visible, the see-er does not appropriate what he sees; he merely approaches it by looking, he opens himself to the world" (Merleau-Ponty, 2000a, p. 162). Restored to art education is a teaching approach that admits "for itself" (Merleau-Ponty, 2000b, p. 69) the student's primal vision and visibility as the advent of their brute meaning. Why should this be so important and what does it further imply for art education?

Merleau-Ponty's reply would be that art education must radiate from the child's first ruminations of the world because these things are an indispensable aspect of their being human, for gaining knowledge of the world and a vital source of their satisfying and developing creative action. It is the human body in its innocence, intensity, silence, excitement, and fragility that negates a mere "outline of being" (Merleau-Ponty, 2000a, p. 161) and "absolute artificialism" (Merleau-Ponty, 2000a, p. 160). It is in the human body, where all the ebb and flow and unrest of art education is taking place as a single, present, and actual being, whose feelings and emanations make a difference in the world as the basis of the child's art education. Merleau-Ponty is claiming that the human body extends vision in a way only the human body can by conversing, transfiguring, surpassing, and transporting the outspread arms of the child whose own momentum hugs the world and kisses it as a conclusion of an inexhaustible self.

If we cannot stand back from the student's artefact on view, we cannot take in what standing back can bring to the inspection of the artwork. In the same way, if I cannot walk around the object, walk towards it, touch and feel it, I will be unable to take up what flows from these experiences. Likewise, of course, vision and visibility is affected by light and the shapes, colours, spatial surroundings and textures of objects to such a degree that "we make perceptions out of the things perceived" (Merleau-Ponty, 2002, p. 5).

Conceived by Merleau-Ponty is how the human body has its own ontogenesis which helps to determine what is appearing in its field of vision at any one time and weld it to other actions and visions. With every mark the student produces, our teacher interrogate with their gaze so that our student is thinking visually as well as conceptually. "The artist can only put down what remains in his head after looking" (Sylvester, 1994, p. 36). Giacometti writes: "When you're making sculpture, it's within reach of our fingers" (Sylvester, 1994, p.127). The activity of seeing, touching, hearing, and moving can bring an attitude of understanding from our student's situation where things can change simply by being moved, touched, heard, or by getting closer to them. The student's gaze "climbs towards the desired form" (Marion, 2004, p.39). These incidents and situations which the child's body gets itself into to magnify their life are the "anchored points" (Merleau-Ponty, 2002, p. 290) for some germane discussions with children and adults. A teacher wants to know how a child-adult is looking.

"In the work of Cézanne, Juan Gris, Braque and Picasso, in different ways, we encounter objects—lemons, mandolins, bunches of grapes, pouches of tobacco— that do not pass quickly before our eyes in the guise of objects we 'know well' but, on the contrary, hold our gaze, ask questions of it, convey to it in a bizarre fashion the very secret of their substance, the very mode of their material existence and which, so to speak, stand 'bleeding' before us. This is how painting led us back to a vision of things themselves" (Merleau-Ponty, 2004, p. 93).

What constitutes 'this bleeding' in art education comes from not "overlooking oneself" (Merleau-Ponty, 2002, p. 207). Because by not 'overlooking oneself' when being immersed in a teaching situation the revelatory expression and gesture of the student's will adopt a 'bleeding' that is unpretending and discerning. The poetic image comes from engaging the child's "sentiment of life" (Merleau-Ponty, 1981a, p. 48) and if in art education we overlook ourselves then what we will be overlooking is how to feel our way spontaneously, attentively, and cleverly. If the student in art is trained to overlook themselves this will lead "to death by an entropy of insignificance" (Marion, 2004, p. 35). The art student's critical actions have "autochthonous meaning" (Merleau-Ponty, 1967, p. 154) and "immanent signification" (Merleau-Ponty, 1967, p. 157) which affects the "flesh of things"

(Merleau-Ponty, 2000, p. 165), the swollen, separated, distorted, and the expanded with a past and a present in the live, producing moment.

"The drawing is no longer to be read the way it was until recently. It is not to be dominated by the look" (Merleau-Ponty, 1981, p. 150) but rather, as Merleau-Ponty goes on to say, by the student's finitude.

IV

'Milk and Milk Bottles': testing out in an art lesson Merleau-Ponty's theory

How might we teach this assignment so that it has clear Merleau-Ponty thinking behind it? Let us take up this challenge. In this final section I want to describe how we can put into practice an art education approach that neither prejudges nor creates a ready-made world of exactly what an art assignment must communicate. What we will need to demonstrate is how we can teach art effectively without circumscribing precisely the learning outcomes for it. If we are to follow Merleau-Ponty's perspective on this, we will want the students to express themselves through their experience of the object(s) as only their "personal apperception" (Merleau-Ponty, 1996, p. 63) can. Crucially, one cannot create an assignment in art which does not include Merleau-Ponty's belief that the student must learn from themselves in meaningful ways. We have previously outlined some of the artistic examples that Merleau-Ponty uses which may help us in the actuality of teaching and we have further outlined sixteen points that are pertinent to the success of teaching an assignment of this kind. We have therefore most of what we would need to design an assignment based on Merleau-Ponty's philosophical ideas.

In my assignment of 'Milk and Milk Bottles' we have set up a painting, drawing, mix-media, photographic, graphic, craft, product design, textiles and sculpture exercise for some fifteen-year-old students based around the theme 'Milk and Milk Bottles'.

One of the first things to mention, in order to teach this project so that it bears the stamp of Merleau-Ponty's thinking, is that it must be taught in a dialogical and open way, involving fundamentally the student who is perceiving. The student is to be encouraged inquisitively to wander and inspect the objects for themselves; this being an assignment that provokes what is seen and reached for in visible ways. A multiplicity of unexpected creations may come from the students when they are "active in their inversions" (Bachelard, 1994, p. xix). For the student's work to succeed they must begin to establish their own immediate relationship with the assignment. They should be invited to express thoroughly the 'object' from their own perspective in relation to a growing, and more confident exploration of seeing what there is from sensory and imaginative reactions and material handling. Derived from the assignment itself the student's way of working is not to reinstate the ordinariness of things themselves, 'this is a milk bottle', with no presence of an "infinite intelligence" (Merleau-Ponty, 2000a, p. 150) attached to it, but what the student can see and express when they plunge themselves into the world of the 'object', the seen and the invisible to reveal what is deeply seated there, waiting to be seen.

As an introduction only, my approach to the problem of art with 'Milk and Milk Bottles' would involve setting up the kind of project where such materials as clay, plaster, wire, metals, fabrics, plastics, leaves, milk, milk bottles, and milk bottle tops, timber, fabric, pastels, crayons, pencils, pen and ink, charcoal, acrylic, gouache, oil paint and watercolours were at hand to be used. This would include paper and sketchbook exercises, maquettes, photographic montage work, and glass-making samples that the students would complete. The reason for the broad range of materials in this project is to offer not only choice without restriction in their use, but when the student draws from the use of such materials to encourage the kind of access which expresses the student's lived experience and the positivity of their expressive vision in art education. The student's gaze wanders and in so doing it just may be the use of fabric by the student which comes to be used in a three-dimensional way rather than in a painting way because the material inspires vision and visibility in a way other materials may not do for them.

Certainly, we all know as teachers that without any contextualising and storytelling, this project of 'Milk and Milk Bottles' will simply fall flat on its face. I will briefly contextualise a little of this project so that we can see how it might help enthuse an interest in 'Milk and Milk Bottles' because the very thing we want students to create in their work is the quality and flesh of things reinforced by personal vision. I would suggest to begin with that the title 'Milk and Milk Bottles' can be taken in all kinds of ways: about milk alone or milk and milk bottles, just milk bottles, or just a milk bottle. The use of students' personal vision to seek out and devour the seen and their interest in it would be stressed from locally present situations.

I have chosen 'Milk and Milk Bottles' as the theme because of students' prior experience. They are inexpensive objects and easily obtainable. They are familiar objects to students, their parents and the world around them. Therefore, as an assignment, our students can quickly produce meaningful results, irrespective of their different abilities in art education. The students already know me as a challenging, and constantly surprising teacher, so anything I am about to do will not seem out of the ordinary. The assignment has been broken down into three sections consisting of photographic work, drawing-painting-mix media work and a craft sculpture-making exercise. I remind the students what we covered and learnt in our last project based on Van Gogh's painting *Boots with Laces* (Paris 1886).

When the students first arrive in the art studio they would see on display a large body of art-related work relating to African, Impressionist, Post Impressionist, Cubist, Futurist, Vorticist, Pop Art, Surrealist, Abstract Expressionist, Conceptual, 'Realist' and photographers' images. Images found in popular magazines corresponding to our theme with some images of dairy cows and glass making would further be included. The point of this large display of work, some 30 or 40 different images in total, is significant because when we come to discuss this work in some detail, the students will survey these images in a manner that caresses and "espouses their contours and their reliefs" (Merleau-Ponty, 2000b, p. 76) as matter spontaneously received. As remarked, one learns from the visible, and only by seeing. When discussing this display of work we do so with knowledge of the visible and vision in mind and without unnecessary constraint we would further discuss how to take this assignment forward.

In the centre of the art studio space a large wooden table has been purposely set up with the range of milk bottles placed on it. The studio in the school has good natural light. I have managed to collect milk bottles from Russia, Turkey, South Africa, USA, Canada, France, Ireland, and the UK. The milk bottles vary in size, colour, shape, texture, ellipses, thickness, embossing, weight, lettering, and transparency. I have some early 19th century milk bottles as well as current milk bottles on display. Some of the bottles are half filled with milk, some are unopened milk bottles, some have dried milk stains on the outside of their shapes, around their rims and as stain marks on the table, some still have the cream on the top of them and some are crystal clear glass bottles. I invite the students to touch, move around the display, hear the sounds they can make and smell the full and empty milk bottles. As I am talking to the students about this assignment I have a pint of milk in my hand that I am occasionally drinking. We spontaneously discuss the visible and invisible qualities of milk and milk bottles.

I ask the students whether they have ever bought a pint of ice cold milk as they walked to school. How does milk differ from water, fizzy drinks, or orange juice? The ritual event of milk at breakfast time is deliberated. The taste of milk, its nutritional value, what foods and drinks have milk in it, like custard, rice pudding, cakes, milkshakes, milk and honey, milk and cookies, hot chocolate, tea, coffee and pancakes and of going to the shops to buy a pint of milk and a newspaper. We talk about what a pint of milk would have cost in the 1940s and what it costs now and who decides its pricing. We debate some of the political controversies that milk has generated and some of the milk marketing board's advertising campaigns. I would further ask the students if any of them worked on a dairy farm milking cows and if they knew how milk bottles were made. I hand out to the group some statistics on milk consumption from different countries in the world. My talk emphasises the visible by perception of the actual objects in situation as well as the visible that they the students might get caught up in that is not physically present in the actual objects but is cemented by a history, a memory, and a conceptual relationship that comes together within a self-determining totality of experience. "What we call a visible is, we said, a quality pregnant with texture, the surface of a depth, a cross-section upon a massive being, a grain or corpuscle borne by a wave of being" (Merleau-Ponty, 2000b, p. 136).

Students are shown photographs of my fridge at home with milk in it and we would discuss these images and its theatre. I ask the students if a milkman delivered milk to their door step or did they get it from the supermarket and the different kinds of milk one can buy. We discuss what would happen to a baby that was not fed on milk. I read to them Henry Munro's poem *Milk for the Cat* and William Butler Yeats' poem, *Spilt Milk*. Finally, together, we exchange views on a selection of the milk and milk bottles on display, mindful of much of their visual appearances, possible messages and evocations. To help the students see more of the visible and invisible, I would use various metaphors, past students' work, and different visual points of views to liberate further how a student might want to take this project forward. As always, I highlighted some of the possible initial drawing, making, and painterly problems that the student may come across when starting a project like this. The point of these discussions, as one can see, is to introduce the student to the various ways a project like this could be taken, the power of an image and what can be experienced when we begin to work on, question, and refine our vision. A glaringly different piece of artwork, in itself, is not what is called for from the student, but instead, to establish the very life of the object in a precious way. So that what is rendered is the 'result of a dehiscence of being'.

It is Friday afternoon and the lesson is finished before the students have even got started. So students have been given a weekend homework assignment to produce a minimum of eight different photographic images relating to our theme, and to produce some notes on the project in their sketchbook. We have a dark room in the art studio area and we have two computers with a printer available for the hard copies of digital images that are needed. The project has been discussed as a spectacle. We covered some of the representational, poetic, expressive, theatrical, conceptual, domestic, industrial, social, and realistic issues. Students are to tell their own story by sensitising themselves to the challenges of the assignment. In dialogue with the student we discussed how the milk bottles on the table seem to "strike our eyes and attack our senses" (Merleau-Ponty, 1996, p. 61).

There will be much more to discuss in the project as we progress through it. For now, the project details and its images are on the school's website, including previous year's work which students can access at any time. As I sip some of the last drops of milk from the bottle the students leave with a handout that has all the project details in it. What I have done so far in this assignment is to vividly present some of the possible life qualities of the visible, answered concerns, and with it what the students aiming of the 'Milk and Milk Bottles should be: the production of the students' own apperception in visually perceptive ways. So that as a teacher I might feel, for instance, in the presence of their artwork "the texture of the sleek and the rough" (Merleau-Ponty, 2000, p. 166).

In an assignment like this we have to distance ourselves, as mentioned, from trouble-free vision, standardisation, and predictability. Why so? Bertrand Russell's description, for example, of a table, though perceptually correct in one sense, is hardly conducive to the exigent self-determining way of how perception and experience operates in art education. "To the eye it is oblong, brown and shiny; to the touch it is smooth and cool and hard; when I tap it, it gives a wooden sound" (Russell, 1919, p. 11). What we have here is articulation without depth, a perception with limited imagination, a melting of vision without danger or desire. Does it follow that the student's self-producing world of art is necessarily any less real than the table that is in front of them which they can tap with their hand? Is Russell's picture of a table an inattentive depiction of what "my impassioned gaze can see" (Marion, 2004, p.56)? The student's ability to produce their own image of a table may be the kind of thing that can be found in the world as soon as it exists. Thus, an image constructed by the student's experience may relate to our perceptual world as something proper to ourselves and the world (Todes, 2001, p.142–3). Russell's notion of a table is too passive and ineffective for use in art education. There is no passion expressed in Russell's observation. Seeing of this kind appears to be reduced to a "seeing apparatus" (Marion, 2004, p. 37), an impersonal being. If we were to take up Russell's account of a table, the art lesson would overrule creative work, vision and visibility, where things begin to stir in a personal felt moment. Art education thrives on immediacy, however. Educationally missing is the particular, as well as the student's orientation, self-moving experience, and situation, delicate gestures and the expression that the object means something beyond creating a diagram of it. Russell's remark at one level is faultless but at another level bare and independent of the actuality and capacity of a self "in our self" (Todes, 2001, p. 174). It is bare because it achieves nothing that would be seen as poetically valuable and appears to use the body's consciousness and imaginative world in the most minimum and rigid of ways. Merleau-Ponty quotes Jean Paulhan: "the space of modern painting is 'space which the heart feels', space in which we too are located, space which is close to us and with which we are organically connected" (Merleau-Ponty, 2004, p. 54).

Disconcertedly, Russell thinks the painter is not interested in knowing what things are (Russell, 1919, p.13). This has been a prevalent notion in philosophic thinking but importantly for education, a teacher of art notes that "since the world of our imagination is nothing but ourselves as imaginative subjects, all our activity productive of images in the world of our imagination, is activity internal to ourselves" (Todes, 2001, p. 142) and the world. Imagination and perception, as Todes deduces, are with us in the world and are essential functions for finding ourselves and determining some things that are presented to our experiences. For Russell, defining the object takes precedence over the "passionate liaison of our bodies" (Bachelard, 1994, p. 15). Thus, he is keen to separate things from the way they might appear (Merleau-Ponty, 2004, p. 94) to the student in what the visual might give in experience. As Merleau-Ponty proclaims:

"*Of course, when I give a dictionary definition of a table—a horizontal flat surface supported by three or four legs, which can be used for eating off, reading a book on, and so forth—I may feel that I have got, as it were, to the essence of the table; I withdraw my interest from all the accidental properties which may accompany that essence, such as the shape of the feet, the style of the moulding and so on*" (Merleau-Ponty, 2004, p. 94).

Referring to Jean-Paul Sartre's *Being and Nothingness*, Merleau-Ponty writes that each attribute such as the shape of the feet "'reveals the being' of the object" (Merleau-Ponty, 2004, p. 62). Hence, if our student is interested in how the glass of the milk bottles is attracting, absorbing, bending space, holding, distorting, turning, and reflecting light, these perceptions when explored in actual practice, can help to recapture and judge an object like this in sensuous or other in ways. This spectacle is part of the presence that reveals the milk bottles and the way our students decipher their qualities (Sartre, 1984, p. 186). Because there are multiple ways in which our Milk and Milk Bottles assignment can be explored, Merleau-Ponty is adamant that we should not predetermine the course and the outcome of the art production, when a project like this is being governed by actual perceptions shaped by their context and local stimuli. We are invited to go back and experience for ourselves all that we can encounter in the visual field that integrates the realm of our own understanding about the object as signs with amplify the sophistication of our perceptions. Art education explores the active experience of the student as the real thing which above all else subsequently determines the appearance of the artwork at any one time.

In teaching this Milk and Milk Bottles assignment, I have wanted the students to transcend the object's 'frontal properties'. So that the student "searches not for the outside of movement but for its secret ciphers" (Merleau-Ponty, 2000a, p. 186) subject to their experience-knowledge. This secret cipher for Merleau-Ponty is evident in how Matisse's women "were not immediate women; they became women. It is Matisse who taught us to see their contours" (Merleau-Ponty, 2000a, p. 184). Hence, we teach our students in an assignment like this to learn how to break the "skin of things" (Merleau-Ponty, 2000a, p. 181), an operation that involves getting beneath what they casually see to achieve something more discreet.

Unquestionably, the key to art practice in education is to capitalise on the "promiscuity between the seeing and the seen" (Merleau-Ponty, 2000a, p. 171), vision and visibility. The student body inhabits, dwells, and "extends towards things, this primary here from which all there's will come (Merleau-Ponty, 2000a, p. 175). To judge an object and dwell in it will require a grip on those perceptions that provide the student with a field of presence linking the subject matter to its space and situation. It will also require from the student the ability to realise and return them to appearances which guide them to a re-landscaping of their object.

From Merleau-Ponty's phenomenology we have constructed a teaching assignment to show how it is possible in an art class or studio to support the student's creative life while deepening their vision and visibility that refers to their open experience of the seen that implies its character. Variations of what can be accomplished by the seen have been discussed. We have further considered "how vision alone makes us learn that beings that are different, exterior to one another, are yet absolutely together" (Merleau-Ponty, 2000a, p. 187). We have examined "what vision can teach us" (Merleau-Ponty, 2000a, p. 187). In this manner, the receptivity of vision and visibility and the giving of oneself to manifest the visible and invisible in situational ways is also a return to response, projection, and seeing. To what gives in apperception, demands more educational importance and activity than is currently the case. Can we have a social world, a meaningful world, and an art education without what constitutes the "sensible for itself" (Merleau-Ponty, 2000, p. 167), by what appears, and by "making myself a world" (Merleau-Ponty, 2000, p. 167)? Merleau-Ponty believes that education must not turn away from existence. What would be the sense of teaching art without the understood relation of what the body can unite and be caught up in? What indeed would be the sense of teaching art without the genuine sensibilities of the student's look? It seems ludicrous to suggest that we can be teaching art and have a syllabus in art education that was unaware of the million flashes of intelligent looking from vision and movement that could be dancing unseen before our very eyes but which appear to have no determinable consequences for teaching. Merleau-Ponty brings to our attention the essential question of whether education can continue to model itself and deny the relevance for human becoming implied by the content experience and perceptions of students.

REFERENCES

Abbs, P. (1989). *The symbolic order: A contemporary reader on the arts debate*. London, England: Routledge Falmer.

Adler, A. (1970). *The education of children* (E. Jensen, Trans.). Chicago: Henry Regnery Company.

Alexander, T. M. (1987). *John Dewey's theory of art, experience & nature: The horizons of feeling*. Ithaca, NY: State University of New York Press.

Altieri, C. (2001). Wittgenstein on consciousness and language. In R. Allen & M. Turvey (Eds.), *Wittgenstein, theory and the arts*. London, England: Routledge.

Ambrose, A. (Ed.). (2001). *Wittgenstein's lectures, Cambridge 1932–35*. New York: Prometheus Books.

Aristotle. (1984). Metaphysics. In J. Barnes (Ed.), *The complete works of Aristotle*. Princeton, NJ: Princeton University Press.

Aristotle. (1984). Nicomachean ethics. In J. Barnes (Ed.), *The complete works of Aristotle*. Princeton, NJ: Princeton University Press.

Aristotle. (1984). Poetics. In J. Barnes (Ed.), *The complete works of Aristotle*. Princeton, NJ: Princeton University Press.

Aristotle. (1984a). Nicomachean ethics. In J. Barnes (Ed.), *The complete works of Aristotle*. Princeton, NJ: Princeton University Press.

Aristotle. (1984b). Poetics. In J. Barnes (Ed.), *The complete works of Aristotle*. Princeton, NJ: Princeton University Press.

Aristotle. (1984c). Problems. In J. Barnes (Ed.), *The complete works of Aristotle*. Princeton, NJ: Princeton University Press.

Arnheim, R. (1973). Child art and visual thinking. In H. P. Lewis (Ed.), *Child art: the beginning of self-affirmation*. Berkeley, CA: Diablo Press.

Arnheim, R. (1974). *Art and visual perception: A psychology of the creative eye*. Berkeley, CA: University of California Press.

Auerbach, E. (2003). *Mimesis: The representation of reality in western literature* (W. R. Trask, Trans.). Princeton, NJ: Princeton University Press.

Bachelard, G. (1971). *The poetics of reverie, childhood, language and the cosmos*. Boston: Beacon Press.

Bachelard, G. (1994). *The poetics of space* (M. Jolas, Trans.). Boston: Beacon Press.

Bachelard, G. (1994). *The poetics of space* (M. Jolas, Trans.). Boston: Beacon Press.

Bachelard, G. (1994). *The poetics of space* (M. Jolas, Trans.). Boston: Beacon Press.

Bachelard, G. (1994). *The poetics of space* (M. Jolas, Trans.). Boston: Beacon Press.

Barbaras, R. (2004). *The being of the phenomenon: Merleau-Ponty's ontology*. Bloomington, IN: Indiana University Press.

Beardsley, M. C. (1981). *Aesthetics: Problems in the philosophy of criticism*. Indianapolis, IN: Hackett Publishing Co.

Bennett, A. (2006). *The history boys*. London, England: Faber and Faber Inc.

Berger, J. (2002). *The shape of a pocket*. London, England: Bloomsbury Publishing.

Biestra, G. (1995). Pragmatism as pedagogy of communicative action. In J. Garrison (Ed.), *The new scholarship on Dewey*. Dordrecht, Netherlands: Kluwer Academic Publishers.

Blackburn. S. (2007). *Plato's Republic: A biography*. Vancouver, Canada: Douglas & McIntyre.

Broudy, H. S. (1994). *Enlightened cherishing: Essay on aesthetic education*. Chicago: University of Illinois Press.

Budd, M. (1996). *Values of art, pictures, poetry and music*. London, England: Penguin Books.

Cannatella, H. (2004). In defense of observational practice in art and design education. *The Journal of Aesthetic Education, 38*, 65–77.

Caro, A. (2006). Seated woman. In D. Mitchinson (Ed.), *Celebrating Moore: Works from the collection of the Henry Moore foundation*. London, England: Lund Humphries.

REFERENCES

Charlton, W. (2000). Pictorial Likeness. *British Journal of Aesthetics, 40*, 467–478.

Clark, K. (1948). Introduction. In M. Richardson (Ed.), *Art and the child*. London, England: University of London Press.

Cobb, E. (1993). *The ecology of imagination and childhood*. Dallas, TX: Spring Publications.

Collingwood, R. G. (1925). Plato's philosophy of art. *Mind, 134*, 154–172.

Collingwood, R. G. (1958). *The principles of art*. Oxford, England: Oxford University Press.

Comte-Sponville, A. (2005). *The little book of philosophy*. London, England: Vintage.

Comte-Sponville, A. (2005). *The little book of philosophy*. London, England: Vintage.

Conrads, U. (1970). *Programmes and manifestoes on 20th-century architecture* (M. Bullock, Trans.). London, England: Lund Humphries.

Cook, H. C. (1919). *The play way*. London, England: William Heinemann Ltd.

Cordasco, F. (1987). *A brief history of education*. Totowa, NJ: Littlefield, Adams & Co.

Danto, A. C. (1994). *The transfiguration of the commonplace*. Cambridge, MA: Harvard University Press.

Davies, S. (2005). *Music*. In J. Levinson (Ed.), *The Oxford handbook of aesthetics*. Oxford, England: Oxford University Press.

Davies, S. (2005). Music. In J. Levinson (Ed.), *The Oxford handbook of aesthetics*. Oxford, England: Oxford University Press.

De Waelhens, A. (1996). *Merleau-Ponty: Philosopher of painting*. In G. A. Johnson (Ed.), *The Merleau-Ponty aesthetics reader: Philosophy and painting* (M. B. Smith, Trans.). Evanston, IL: Northwestern University Press.

Dewey, J. (1944). *Democracy and education*. New York: The Free Press.

Dewey, J. (1980). *Art as experience*. New York: Perigee Books.

Dewey, J. (1980). *Art as experience*. New York: Perigee Books.

Dewey, J. (1980). *Art as experience*. New York: Perigee Books.

Diamond, C. (1996). The realistic spirit, Wittgenstein, philosophy and the mind. Massachusetts: MIT Press.

Diamond, C. (1996). *The realistic spirit: Wittgenstein philosophy and the mind*. Cambridge, MA: The MIT Press.

Efland, D. A. (1990). *A history of art education, intellectual and social currents in teaching the visual arts*. New York: Teachers College Press.

Eisner, E. W. (2006). *Reimagining schools*. London, England: Routledge.

Eisner, W. E. (2002). *The arts and the creation of mind*. New Haven, CT: Yale University Press.

Ferry, L. (1993). *Homo aestheticus: The invention of taste in the democratic age* (R. De Loaiza, Trans.). Chicago: University of Chicago Press.

Gadamer, H. (1989). *Truth and method* (J. Weinsheimer & D. G. Marshall, Trans.). London, England: Sheed & Ward.

Gadamer, H. (1998). *The relevance of the beautiful and other essays* (R. Bernasconi, Ed.). Cambridge, England: Cambridge University Press.

Gardner, H. (1993). *Creating minds*. New York: Harper Collins Publishers.

Garrison, J. (1999). Dangerous dualism in Siegel's theory of critical thinking: A Deweyan pragmatist responds. *Journal of Philosophy of Education, 33*, 213–232.

Garver, N. (1994). *This complicated form of life: Essay on Wittgenstein*. Chicago: Open Court Publishing Company.

Gaut, B. (2001). *The ethical criticism of art in aesthetics and ethics* (J. Levinson, Ed.). Cambridge, England: Cambridge University Press.

Gaut, B. (2001). The ethical criticism of art. In J. Levinson (Ed.), *Aesthetics and ethics*. Cambridge, England: Cambridge University Press.

Gay, P. (Ed.). (1995). *The Freud reader*. London, England: Vintage.

Goldman, A. (2003). Representation in art. In J. Levinson (Ed.), *The Oxford handbook of aesthetics*. Oxford, England: Oxford University Press.

Gombrich, E. H. (1977). *Art and illlusion: A study in the psychology of pictorial representation.* London, England: Phaidon Press Ltd.

Gombrich, E. H. (1977). *Art and illusion: A study in the psychology of pictorial representation.* London, England: Phaidon Press Ltd.

Gonzalez, J. (2004). *Being alive* (N. Astley, Ed.). Northumberland, England: Bloodaxe Books Ltd.

Gooding, M. (2002). *Patrick Heron.* London, England: Phaidon Press.

Goodman, N. (1986). Art and inquiry. In F. Frascina & C. Harrison (Eds.), *Modern art and modernism.* London, England: The Open University Press.

Goodway, D. (1998a). The politics of Herbert Read. In D. Goodway (Ed.), *Herbert Read reassessed.* Liverpool, England: Liverpool University Press.

Goodway, D. (Ed.). (1998). *Herbert Read reassessed.* Liverpool, England: Liverpool University Press.

Graham, G. (1995). Learning from art. *British Journal of Aesthetics, 35,* 26–37.

Grayling, A. C. (1992). Wittgenstein's influence: Meaning, mind and method. In A. P. Griffiths (Ed.), *Wittgenstein centenary essays.* Cambridge, UK: Cambridge University Press.

Greene, M. (1995). *Releasing the imagination: Essays on education, the arts, and social change.* San Francisco: Jossey-Bass Publishers.

Greene, M. (2001). *Variations on a blue guitar.* New York: Teachers Collage Press.

Hacker, P. M. S. (2001). Wittgenstein and the autonomy of humanistic understanding. In R. Allen & M. Turvey (Eds.), *Wittgenstein, theory and the arts.* London, UK: Routledge.

Hagberg, G. L. (1995). *Art as language: Wittgenstein, meaning, and aesthetic theory.* Ithaca, NY: Cornell University Press.

Halliwell, S. (1998). *Aristotle poetics.* London, England: The University of Chicago Press.

Halliwell, S. (1998). *Aristotle's poetics.* London, England: The University of Chicago Press.

Halliwell, S. (1998). *Aristotle's poetics.* London, UK: University of Chicago Press, Gerald Duckworth & Co. Ltd.

Halliwell, S. (2002). *The aesthetics of mimesis: Ancient texts and modern problems.* Princeton, NJ: Princeton University Press.

Heaney, S. (1979). Feelings into words. In R. Gibbons (Ed.), *The poet's work: 29 masters of 20th century poetry on the origins and practice of their art.* Boston: Houghton Mifflin Company.

Hegel, G. W. F. (1975). *The philosophy of fine art, Vol. 1* (F. P. B. Osmaston, Trans.). New York: Hacker Art Books.

Hegel, G. W. F. (1988). *Hegel's aesthetics* (T. M. Knox, Trans.). Oxford, England: Clarendon Press.

Heidegger, M. (1993). The origin of a work of art. In D. F. Krell (Ed.), *Basic writings.* London, England: Routledge.

Heidegger, M. (2000). The origin of the work of art. In D. Krell (Ed.), *Basic writings.* London, England: Routledge.

Herbert, Z. (1985). *Barbarian in the garden* (M. March & J. Anders, Trans.). London: A Harvest Book, Harcourt Brace & Company.

Herbert, Z. (1985). *Barbarian in the garden* (M. March & J. Anders, Trans.). London, England: A Harvest Book, Harcourt Brace & Company.

Herbert, Z. (1999). *Elegy for the departure and other poems* (J. & B. Carpenter, Trans.). Hopewell, NJ: The Ecco Press.

Irigaray, L. (2002). *The way of love* (H. Bastic & S. Pluháček, Trans.). London, England: Continuum.

Irigaray, L. (2002). *The way of love.* (H. Bostic & S. Pluháček, Trans.). London, England: Continuum.

Jackson, P. W. (1995). If we took Dewey's aesthetics seriously, how would the arts be taught? In J. Garrison (Ed.), *The new scholarship on Dewey.* Dordrecht, Netherlands: Kluwer Academic Publishers.

Jackson, P. W. (1998). *John Dewey and the lessons of art.* New Haven, CT: Yale University Press.

Johannessen, K. S. (2004). Wittgenstein and the aesthetic domain. In P. B. Lewis (Ed.), *Wittgenstein, aesthetics and philosophy.* Aldershot, England: Ashgate Publishing Company.

Kant, I. (1992). *The critique of judgement* (J. C. Meredith, Trans.).Oxford, England: Clarendon Press.

Kant, I. (1992a). *Critique of pure reason* (N. K. Smith, Trans.). London, England: Macmillan Press Ltd.

REFERENCES

Kelly, S. (2003). Merleau-Ponty on the body. In M. Proudfoot (Ed.), *The philosophy of body*. Oxford, England: Blackwell Publishing.

Kemp, M. (1989). Art and imagination. In *Leonardo Da Vinci*. London, England: Hayward Gallery.

Lefort, C. (2000). Forward. In M. Merleau-Ponty (Ed.), *The visible and the invisible*. Evanston, IL: Northwestern University Press.

Leonardo Da Vinci. (1989). London, England: Hayward Gallery.

Livingston, M. (1994). *Jim Dine flowers and plants*. New York: Harry. N. Abrams, Inc. Publishers.

Lowenfeld, V., & Brittain, W. L. (1982). *Creative and mental growth*. New York: Macmillan Publishing Co Inc.

Lucie-Smith, E. (2002). *Art tomorrow*. Paris, France: Editions Pierre Terrail.

Lyotard, J. (1984). *The postmodern condition: A report on knowledge, theory and history of literature: Vol. 10* (G. Bennington & B. Massumi, Trans.). Minneapolis, MN: University of Minnesota Press.

Malraux, A. (1990). *The voices of silence* (S. Gilbert, Trans.). Princeton, NJ: Princeton University Press.

Malvern, S. B. (1995). Inventing 'child' art: Franz Cizek and modernism. *British Journal of Aesthetics, 35*, 262–272.

Marion, J. (2004). *The crossing of the visible* (J. K. A. Smith, Ed.). Stanford, CA: Stanford University Press.

Marion, J. (2004). *The crossing of the visible* (J. K. A. Smith, Trans.). Stanford, CA: Stanford University Press.

Merleau-Ponty, M. (1967). *The structure of behaviour* (A. L. Fisher, Trans.). London, England: Beacon Press.

Merleau-Ponty, M. (1981). Expression and the child's drawing. In J. Wild (Ed.), *The prose of the world*. Evanston, IL: Northwestern University Press.

Merleau-Ponty, M. (1981a). The indirect language. In J. Wild (Ed.), *The prose of the world*. Evanston, IL: Northwestern University Press.

Merleau-Ponty, M. (1996). Cézanne's doubt. In G. A. Johnson (Ed.), *The Merleau-Ponty aesthetics reader* (M. B. Smith, Trans.). Evanston, IL: Northwestern University Press.

Merleau-Ponty, M. (1996). Cézanne's Doubt. In G. A. Johnson (Ed.), *The Merleau-Ponty aesthetics reader: Philosophy and painting* (M. B. Smith, Trans.). Evanston, IL: Northwestern University Press.

Merleau-Ponty, M. (2000). The intertwining-the chiasm. In C. Cazeaux (Ed.), *The continental aesthetics reader*. London, England: Routledge.

Merleau-Ponty, M. (2000). *The visible and the invisible* (J. Wild, Ed.). Evanston, IL: Northwestern University Press.

Merleau-Ponty, M. (2000a). *The primacy of perception* (J. Wild, Ed.). Evanston, IL: Northwestern University Press.

Merleau-Ponty, M. (2000b). *The visible and the invisible* (J. Wild, Ed.). Evanston, IL: Northwestern University Press.

Merleau-Ponty, M. (2002). *Phenomenology of perception* (C. Smith, Trans.). London, England: Routledge.

Merleau-Ponty, M. (2004). *The world of perception* (D. Oliver, Trans.). London, England: Routledge.

Merleau-Ponty, M. (2004). *The world of perception* (O. Davis, Trans.). London, England: Routledge.

Monk, R. (1991). *Ludwig Wittgenstein: The duty of genius*. London, England: Vintage.

Moore, H., & Hedgecoe, J. (1986). *Henry Moore, my ideas, inspiration and life as an artist*. London, England: Ebury Press.

Moore, H., & Hedgecoe, J. (1986). *Henry Moore: My ideas, inspiration and life as an Artist*. London, UK: Ebury Press.

Moran, D. (2000). *Introduction to phenomenology*. London, England: Routledge.

Moravcsik, J. (1982). Poetic aspiration and artistic inspiration. In J. Moravcsik & P. Temko (Eds.), *Plato on beauty, wisdom and the arts*. Totowa, NJ: Rowman Littlefield.

Nehamas, A. (1982). Plato on imitation and poetry in Republic 10. In J. Moravcsik & P. Temko (Eds.), *Plato on beauty, wisdom and the arts*. Totowa, NJ: Rowman Littlefield.

Nemerov, H. (2002). The painter dreaming in the scholar's house. In N. Astley (Ed.), *Staying alive*. Northumberland, England: Bloodaxe Books.

Nietzsche, F. (1968). *The will to power* (W. Kaufman, Ed., W. Kaufmann & R. J. Hollingdale, Trans.). New York: Vintage Books.

Nowlan, A. (2004). He sits down on the floor of a school for the retarded. In *Between tears and laughter*. Northumberland, England: Bloodaxe Books Ltd.

Nussbaum, M. C. (1992). *Love's knowledge: Essays on philosophy and literature*. Oxford, England: Oxford University Press.

Osborne, H. (1986). Professor Louis Arnaud Reid. *British Journal of Aesthetics, 26*, 309–310.

Pears, D. (1988). *The false prison: A study of the development of Wittgenstein's philosophy: Volume two*. Oxford, UK: Clarendon Press.

Perry, L. R. (1992). *Notebook, thoughts on the curriculum*. London, England: University of London, Institute of Education.

Peters, M. (2000). Writing the self: Wittgenstein, confession and pedagogy. *Journal of Philosophy of Education, 34*, 353–368.

Peters, M., & Marshall, J. (1999). *Wittgenstein: Philosophy, postmodernism, pedagogy* (H. A. Giroux, Ed.). Westport, CT: Bergin & Garvey.

Plato. (1997). Laws. In D. S. Hutchinson (Ed.), *Plato complete works*. Indianapolis, IN: Hackett Publishing Co, Inc.

Plato. (1997a). Parmenides. In D. S. Hutchinson (Ed.), *Plato complete works*. Indianapolis, IN: Hackett Publishing Co, Inc.

Plato. (1997b). Republic. In D. S. Hutchinson (Ed.), *Plato complete works*. Indianapolis, IN: Hackett Publishing Co, Inc.

Read, B., & Thistlewood, D. (Eds.). (1994). *Herbert Read: A British vision of world art*. London, England: Lund Humphries Publishers Limited.

Read, H. (1944). *The education of free men*. London, England: Free Press.

Read, H. (1966). *The redemption of the robot: My encounter with education through art*. New York: Trident Press.

Read, H. (1970a). *Education through art*. London, England: Faber and Faber.

Read, H. (1973). Art as a unifying principle in education. In H. P. Lewis (Ed.), *Child art: The beginning of self-affirmation*. Berkeley, CA: Diablo Press.

Read. H. (1970). *Art and society*. New York: Schocken Books.

Read. H. (2002). *To hell with culture*. London, England: Routledge Classics.

Reid, L. A. (1961). *Ways of knowledge and experience*. London, England: George Allen & Unwin Ltd.

Reid, L. A. (1969). *Meaning in the arts*. London, England: George Allen and Unwin Ltd.

Reid, L. A. (1973). *A study in aesthetics*. Conneticut, CT: Greenwood Press, Publishers.

Reid, L. A. (1983). *The conceptual understanding of art and the aesthetic; their importance for education in art and design education: Heritage and prospect, Bedford Way Papers, No. 14* (A. Dyson, Ed.). London, England: Institute of Education.

Reid, L. A. (1989). *The arts within a plural concept of knowledge in the symbolic order: A contemporary reader on the arts debate* (P. Abbs, Ed.). London, England: Routledge Falmer.

Richardson, M. (1948). *Art and the child*. London, England: University of London Press Ltd.

Richardson, M. (1948). *Art and the child*. London, England: University of London Press.

Richter, G. (1995). *The daily practice of painting, writings and interviews 1962-1993* (H. U. Obrist, Ed.). Cambidge, MA: The MIT Press.

Rollo, M. (1972). *Power and innocence: A search for the sources of violence*. New York: W.W. Norton & Company Inc.

Rosen, S. (2005). *Plato's republic: A study*. New Haven, CT: Yale University Press.

Ross, M. (1987). Louis Arnaud Reid. *British Journal of Aesthetics, 27*, 101–103.

Ross, M. (1998). Herbert Read: Art, education and the means of redemption. In D. Goodway (Ed.), *Herbert Read reassessed*. Liverpool, England: Liverpool University Press.

REFERENCES

Ross, M., & Mitchell, S. (1993). Assessing achievement in the arts. *British Journal of Aesthetics, 33,* 99–112.

Rousseau, J. (2003). *Émile* (W. H. Payne, Trans.). New York: Prometheus Books.

Russell, B. (1919). *The problems of philosophy.* London, England: Williams and Norgate.

Russell, B. (2002). Introduction. In L. Wittgenstein (Ed.), *Tractatus logico-philosophicus* (D. F. Pears & B. F. McGuinness, Trans.). London, England: Routledge.

Sartre, J. (1984). *Being and nothingness* (H. E. Barnes, Trans.). London, England: Methuen & Co. Ltd.

Sartwell, C. (1992). Realism. In D. Cooper (Ed.), *A companion to aesthetics.* Oxford, England: Basil Blackwell Ltd.

Scarry, E. (2000). *On beauty and being just.* London, England, Gerald Duckworth and Co. Ltd.

Schaeffer, J. M. (2000). *Art of the modern age: Philosophy of art from Kant to Heidegger* (S. Rendall, Trans.). Princeton, NJ: Princeton University Press.

Schiller, F. (1982). *On the aesthetic education of man* (E. M. Wilkinson & L. A. Lilloughby, Trans. & Eds.). Oxford, England: Clarendon Press.

Schiller, F. (2006). *Aesthetical and philosophical essays.* Middlesex, England: The Echo Library.

Scruton, R. (1982). *Art and imagination: Study in the philosophy of mind.* London, England: Routledge & Kegan Paul.

Shusterman, R. (1995). Popular art and education. In J. Garrison (Ed.), *The new scholarship on Dewey.* Dordrecht, Netherlands: Kluwer Academic Publishers.

Stallabrass, J. (2006). Woman seated on a stool. In D. Mitchinson (Ed.), *Celebrating Moore: works from the collection of the Henry Moore foundation.* London, England: Lund Humphries.

Stern, A. (1973). The child's language of art. In H. P. Lewis (Ed.), *Child art: The beginning of self-affirmation.* Berkeley, CA: Diablo Press.

Sylvester, D. (1987). *Interviews with Francis Bacon.* London, England: Thames and Hudson.

Sylvester, D. (1994). *Looking at Giacometti.* New York: Henry Holt and Company.

Tanner, M. (2003). *Ethics and aesthetics are—?* In J. L. Bermúdez & S. Gardner (Eds.), *Art and morality.* London, England: Routledge.

Taylor, C. (1997). *To follow a rule in philosophical arguments.* Cambridge, MA: Harvard University Press.

Todes, S. (2001). *Body and world.* Cambridge, MA: The MIT Press.

Todes, S. (2001). *Body and world.* Cambridge, MA: The MIT Press.

Todes, S. (2001). *Body and world.* Cambridge, MA: The MIT Press.

Todes, S. (2001). *Body and world.* Cambridge, MA: The MIT Press.

Valéry, P. (1989). *The art of poetry* (J. Mathews, Ed., D. Folliot, Trans.). Princeton, NJ: Princeton University Press.

Viola, W. (1936). *Child art and Franz Cizek.* Vienna, Austria: Austrian Junior Red Cross.

Wegner, C. (1992). *The discipline of taste and feeling.* Chicago: The University of Chicago Press.

White, J. (1995). *Education and personal well-being in a secular universe.* London, England: Institute of Education.

Wiles, S., Dine, J., & Katz, V. (2005). *Jim Dine: Some drawings.* Gottingen, Germany: Steidl Verlag.

Winch, P. (1992). Certainty and authority. In A. P. Griffiths (Ed.), *Wittgenstein centenary essays.* Cambridge, England: Cambridge University Press.

Wittgenstein, L. (1984). *Culture and value* (G. H. Von Wright & H. Nyman, Eds., P. Winch, Trans.). Chicago: The University of Chicago Press.

Wittgenstein, L. (1989). *Philosophical investigations* (G. E. M. Anscombe, Trans.). Oxford, England: Basil Blackwell Ltd.

Wittgenstein, L. (1990). *Last writings on the philosophy of psychology* (Vol. 1, G. E. M. Anscombe & G. H. von Wright, Eds., G. E. M. Anscombe, Trans.). Oxford, England: Basil Blackwell Ltd.

Wittgenstein, L. (1990a). *Remarks on colour* (G. E. M. Anscombe, Ed., L. L. McAlister & M. Schättle, Trans.). Oxford, England: Basil Blackwell Ltd.

Wittgenstein, L. (1990b). *Remarks on the philosophy of psychology* (Vol. 1, G. E. M. Anscome & G. H. von Wright, Eds., G. E. M. Anscome, Trans.). Oxford, England: Basil Blackwell Ltd.

Wittgenstein, L. (1993). *Last writings on the philosophy of psychology* (Vol. 2, G. E. M. Anscombe & G. H. von Wright, Eds., G. E. M. Anscombe, Trans.). Oxford, England: Basil Blackwell Ltd.

Wittgenstein, L. (1993a). *On certainty* (G. E. M. Anscombe & G. H. Von Wright, Eds.). Oxford, England: Basil Blackwell Ltd.

Wittgenstein, L. (1993b). *The blue and brown books: Preliminary studies for the philosophical investigations*. Oxford, England: Basil Blackwell Ltd.

Wittgenstein, L. (1994). *Ludwig Wittgenstein: Lectures and conversations on aesthetic, psychology and religious belief* (C. Barrett, Ed.). Oxford, England: Basil Blackwell Ltd.

Wittgenstein, L. (2002). *Tractatus logico-philosophicus* (D. F. Pears & B. F. McGuinness, Trans.). London, England: Routledge.

Wollheim, R. (1998). *Painting as an art*. London, England: Thames and Hudson.

Wordsworth, W. (1907). Essay, supplementary to the preface. In T. Hutchinson (Ed.), *The poetical works of William Wordsworth*. Oxford, England: Oxford University Press.

Wordsworth, W. (1907). *The poetic works of William Wordsworth* (T. Hutchinson, (Ed.). London, England: Oxford University Press.

Zaslove, J. (1998). Herbert Read and essential modernism: Or the loss of an image of the world. In D. Goodway (Ed.), *Herbert Read reassessed*. Liverpool, England: Liverpool University Press.